A Priest in Changing Times

Memories and Opinions
of
Michael O'Carroll C.S.Sp.

the columba press

First published in 1998 by
the columba press
55a Spruce Avenue, Stillorgan Industrial Park
Blackrock, Co Dublin

Cover by Bill Bolger
Origination by The Columba Press
Printed in Ireland by Colour Books Ltd, Dublin

ISBN 1 85607 229 0

Contents

To St Joseph, Patron of Workers,
and to
Blackrock College, past, present and future

Preface

I hope that the memories I have set forth may be for my readers a stimulus to hope. I tell of good people and of the good in people. As will be evident in the pages which follow, I have encountered those suffering from the evil in others. To dismiss such things or to overlook them through studied indifference would be unpardonable. As I state in my book, I visited Auschwitz prison camp. Like others who have had this painful experience, I feel almost a sacred duty to the victims of what John Paul II called the 'Golgotha of our times', a duty of remembrance, of witness, of prayer. It is to help people who carry a similar burden from one or other ordeal in life, intimate or shared with others, that I publish my memoirs.

I wish to thank my family friends, Margaret O'Donnell of Mary Immaculate College, Limerick, and her sister Dr Máire, for reading the text and helping to eliminate items which disfigured it.

Michael O'Carroll C.S.Sp.
8 December 1997
Feast of the Immaculate Conception of the Blessed Virgin Mary

1. Early Days

I was born on 11 June 1911, in Newcastle West, Co Limerick. My father was Michael Carroll – we later took the 'O' – then a member of the RIC. He had been a sergeant in Strand, not far from Newcastle West. My mother, Hannah Dore from Templeglantine but living in Newcastle for some time, had noticed him with admiration at a funeral They met in Ballybunion some time later with a mutual friend. My father made her a present saying: 'It may lead to greater things.' After a very proper courtship they were engaged and married. I hope that Our Lady was directly involved in this union. I was told many years later that my father, as a young police officer, had given a picture of Our Lady of Perpetual Help to the church in Monegay, near Strand.

My mother dominated my childhood. Since my father was away in his police barracks, the years that I had with her now appear to me precious. Under God she gave me the faith; I did not get it from theologians.She taught me to say the Rosary but, above all, she taught me, by example, the importance of the Mass; she was a daily Mass-goer.I and my two brothers, Patrick and Maurice, were altar-servers. This brought us inside the clerical establishment, gave us familiarity with the liturgy and raised the desirability of the priesthood as an option.

As altar-servers we had exciting moments. Tenebrae, the evening office of Holy Week, was fascinating. Priests came, mostly on horseback, from outlying parishes to participate and the chanting of the psalms was magic; as was the moment when all but one of the lights were extinguished. The altar boy with the one surviving light went behind the altar, leaving all in darkness. The priests clapped on their breviaries, the candle was brought back, and the ceremony ended.

The RIC and the War of Independence

We are now in the days of the war of independence. My father, who was a serious reader with a valuable private library, was self-educated. He had qualified as an Inspector of Weights and Measures and was eventually promoted Head Constable. He was assigned to Bray and should then have been given the rank of District Inspector.This promotion, entirely merited, he was denied. This injustice rankled with him all through life. One explanation was that he was a daily Mass-goer. But he had prosecuted friends of the District Inspector for offences against the liquor laws, and this officer, his immediate superior, may have spoken against him. We thought that as District Inspector his life might have been in danger in the years of conflict. He was posted to Enniskillen and finally to Dunmore, Co Galway. I must record that anyone whom I met who had known him spoke of him with respect. Apart from the sense of injustice he had no scarred memories.

This leads to the problem of the RIC in the war of independence. It is a controversial theme, but I must deal with it. My father was a law enforcement officer, to use the current phrase. He had no interest in politics. When he joined the force his intention was to maintain law and order within the existing system. A de facto government has rights and duties and he served a de facto government. His brothers and first cousin fought in the first world war, as did thousands of their fellow-countrymen. Through the priesthood and religious life, he was intimately part of Irish Cathollc society. Two of his sons became priests; two of his sisters were Marist nuns. It may now be too late to undertake an interesting statistical survey of all those in the priesthood and religious life who were related to members of the RIC. From samples I have taken, the overall picture would be surprising;it would include some prominent intellectuals among the clergy and some bishops.

When the war of independence broke out, the opening episode and a continuous element of the programme was the shooting of members of the police force. They who were, in words once spoken by Eamon de Valera to a friend of mine, Seamus Wilmot, 'a very decent body of men', highly disciplined, often enjoying popular respect, suddenly were depicted as enemies of their country. They were all Irishmen. They were to suffer from the blunders of the British government. Of these, undeniably, the worst was the decision to reinforce their numbers by the Black and Tans, whose conduct shocked the world. My father found some of them cowardly. The force suffered from propaganda, which, in the heat of conflict, had little time for distinctions. Some resigned, whether from honourable motives or fear; some wavered in discipline; some, like my father, kept their ideals and refused to compromise. I am quite sure he retired, when the post-Treaty changeover took place, with his honour intact.

The last year of his service was a strain on my mother.Her cousin and lifelong friend, Michael Dore, a pharmaceutical chemist and my godfather, was very much identified with the nationalist cause. His son, Miceal, assures me that he was not a member of the I.R.A. I had always thought so because on one occasion he was privy to their plans, plans which fortunately did not materialise. Things changed about us in our little world as they did everywhere in the country. Michael Dore, I had been told, had danced with joy at my mother's wedding. He had not lost his respect for my father, nor his affection for my mother, but there was a gap. Cousins of my mother, well-known in West Limerick, the Cregans of Ballyshane, Newcastle West, were out 'on the hills'.

One thing did not change, my mother's generous hospitality; our house was open to all those from the Templeglantine area who were 'in town'. One of our friends, not very much older than me, remarked to me years later that he seemed to drink endless cups of tea at my mother's hand. His name, David ('Dave') Neligan – Michael Collins' 'Spy in the Castle'. His father was the principal of Templeglantine National School and his mother and mine were born and raised in houses side by side in the townland of Doonakenna. Dave would be a Colonel in the first Irish National Army, then head of the CID. My friendship with him was warm into his last years, when he lived in Booterstown, near Blackrock College.

In our town we had little immediate experience of the war of independence. Many townsfolk went on Sunday afternoons to see a soccer match between the Auxiliaries and the 'Tans'. We saw these roaring out towards the country in their Crossley Tenders. I have a distinct memory of one evening when they were clearing the town of country folk; the cry rang out 'Fire ... you,fire'. There was no action. One member of the RIC was shot dead outside the town. A creamery was burned down in reprisal. That was all.

Mother's last days

Against that backdrop we lived our family life. My mother, who would die young, suffered terribly from migraine. I have memories of her in agony, asking me to get a box of starch, which relieved her. I do so wish that I had known her in her early days when she was a glowing tall personality with a head of golden hair, her laughter a tonic. When she became terminally ill, there was a mistaken diagnosis; she was doomed. Her dear friend, Margaret Dee, who was devoted to her, told me that her constant cry was: 'What will become of my children?'

One day when I went to see her she asked me touchingly did I think I would get on with my auntie; she knew that we would leave Newcastle West after her death and go to live with my father's mother and sister. She did not think that she should conceal the certainty of her death from me, though I was then only ten years of age. She did not fear death. Her freedom from such fear was, I think, a grace, straight from the Sacred Heart of Jesus; she had some time previously asked a curate in the town, Fr John Kelly, to consecrate our family to the Adorable Heart of the Saviour.

There are people to whom death comes as a fact only after decades of their life. Mgr Ronald Knox was forty years of age when he saw a corpse for the first time. Aunt Mary, who lived with us, had predeceased my mother by three weeks. She had insisted on burial in the Dore plot in Monegay, some miles outside the town. There was in Newcastle West a new cemetery. I still hear my mother saying at the time: 'What does it matter where you are buried?' It was the soul that counted. Now, as she approached her own departure from this life, she changed her opinion. She wished to be buried in Monegay with the Dores. Thus it was done. It was my fourth funeral as a child, for my godmother, Margaret ('Poll') MacCarthy, had died shortly before, as had a relative of hers who was well known to us.

That my mother has cared for me constantly has been one of the certainties of my life. Many years later I accompanied a group of Belgian pilgrims to Garabandal. At a break in the return journey, I celebrated Mass for the pilgrims. Afterwards, one of those present came to me and said: 'I saw your mother beside you at the altar.' This did not surprise me.

When I think of what some children have suffered, and suffer at the present time, I should not dare say that I had a hard childhood. I was twice a child in a single parent family and probably saw more of life than many children in that age of domestic security.

My mother died on 5 May 1922, aged forty-four. After the death we changed residence and went to live in the village of Jamestown, near Carrick on Shannon. Locality and people were a contrast to what we had experienced until then. With the exception of one maternal aunt, Ellen, married to Edward Bresnihan and living in the old home in Templeglantine, we had had no immediate relatives in Co Limerick; but we had distant cousins and kinsfolk. In Co Leitrim the family was bare of any ties.

Jamestown is on the Shannon, a delightful spot; the people whom I got to know have left me with the happiest memories. There is history in it, and some links with the Williamite war. There were in the neighbourhood a number of 'Big Houses'.One in the village itself, Jamestown House, had been the residence of the O'Beirnes, who had given the Catholic chapel to the inhabitants. One member of this family, Hugh O'Beirne, became famous as a British diplomat in eastern Europe. He died at sea on the Hampshire with Kitchener, on his way to take up the post of British Ambassador to Czarist Russia.

Primary school

My mother had begun my schooling at the Mercy Convent in Co Limerick, where she had formerly taught domestic economy, as it was then called. She had literally to carry me, as I was recalcitrant. After some years I went to the Courtney National School, which had just got a new headmaster, a newcomer to the town, M. B. O'Donnell. The teachers by their personality were educational, for they were highly individual. One was a born educator, Joseph ('Joe') Shea. He was the first teacher I met who inspired me. He encouraged some of his pupils to go on walks with him to study plant life in relation to what we had learned in class. I still remember the excitement of walking along the river banks with him, sharing his interest, almost enthusiasm, in nature.

When we moved to Co Leitrim, I made acquaintance with two more National Schools, one run by the Presentation Brothers in Carrick, which meant a daily walk of over three miles. When that proved too much for me, it was Drumsna National School, to which I walked more than one and a half miles. There was a National School in Jamestown, across the road from our house, with a splendid teacher, Mrs O'Gorman; but it was co-ed, which must have been unique in Ireland at the time; this my father would not have. As I went later to live with my maternal aunt in Templeglantine, I sampled my fifth primary school in that parish, again with a daily walk of a mile or so.

My brothers

Life was not easy for my father. He was forced into retirement at an age when he was at the peak of his ability and energy. He had the joy of seeing two of his sons priests. My elder brother, Patrick, entered the Holy Ghost Congregation. He graduated with a doctorate from the Gregorian University in Rome in 1937 and was immediately appointed Director of Scholastics (i.e. seminarists) in Kimmage. Here he succeeded Fr Edward Leen as Superior of the community and finally was named Provincial, which post he held for nine years.

Fr Pat handed over to a friend of his, Fr Timothy O'Driscoll, a native of Valentia. To leave the way clear he decided to work with our priests in the United States – his health would not support the strain of work in the African missions. He then did the honorable thing – he joined the American province of the Congregation and took out American citizenship. When Pat went to swear his allegiance to the Constitution, he met an official with a sense of humour. 'You better read that before you swear it,' he was told. Pat came to the sentence, 'I will answer the call to defend this country under arms if summoned.' He turned to the official: 'May I make a statement sir?' 'Sure, father.' 'I'll come if you send for me, but I don't think I'll be of much use to you.' 'May I make a statement, father? I don't think we'll send for you.'

On visits to the US, I was happy to see that Pat was most welcome to our American colleagues; they insisted on having him superior of community though he was FBI (Foreign born Irish).He had been ill all through the summer of 1967 when I was in Kenya. But in the autumn I finally had word from him that he was out of hospital and things looked well. That same night I was called to the telephone by one of his great friends who said that he had collapsed, was back in hospital and the doctor was holding out no hope. I spoke at once to my Provincial, Fr Vincent Dinan. 'You must go out at once, Michael.'

This I did. Though the nurse attending him had told me while I was in Dublin that there was little hope, he rallied and, perhaps through the effect of revived childhood memories, he seemed to recover.He was fortunate in the nurses: the Jewish and Protestant nurses showed how they would serve a Catholic priest, and the Catholics were 'all out'. His doctor was Jewish, totally competent and careful. Pat had a number of Jewish friends who were so generous to me. I was advised that he might live on, so I came home to my work; five days later I was called to the telephone to hear of his death. A sign of the love for him: the priest who spoke the homily at his funeral broke down and left the pulpit in tears.

My other brother, Maurice, had returned to Templeglantine to work the family farm. Life was not easy for him; he too was to die young. He was with me when our father died, and was buried in Jamestown.

My father's last years

My father married a second time, late in life, a lady much younger than him. Her devotion to her husband was total, as was that of their only child, Edward. My father died on 23 April 1961, in his ninetieth year; it was the Patrician year and it was the feast of St George. He had been a daily Mass-goer all his life. In the Jamestown years this meant more than a mile and a half every morning; later in the day he went to make the Stations of the Cross. He carried beyond the grave memories of lifelong fidelity to the faith. As a very young man he had honoured Our Lady of Knock soon after the apparition, travelling there by bicycle. He was there on 18 August 1940 when I was the celebrant of the Mass, the culmination of nationwide prayers and Masses for the protection of Ireland during the war. He was present in St Peter's square in Rome, on 1 November 1950 when Pius XII defined the dogma of the Assumption. He received special graces in his last years. When I visited him shortly before his death his serenity, lucidity and joy were awesome.

The dear old man was worried that, as had happened with other members of the RIC, there would be no reference in the death notice to his membership of the force. Since, through the absence of my elder brother in the United States, I had to see to these matters, I respected his wishes fully, following my own deep instinct also.

My father was a man of honour and he was indifferent to what people thought or said of him. I pray that I be worthy of such a precious legacy.

Secondary School

I came to Blackrock College in 1924. I was in what was then called the Junior Scholasticate, a junior seminary which was part of the whole secondary school. Apart from worship and study we were part of the college, one with them in the celebration of important liturgical events, in games and entertainment, in class and student activities like debating societies. We were all friends and I followed the fortunes of my classmates in later life. Two were decorated for military valour in World War II: Michael Murray, a captain in the Irish Guards, got the M.C. in the Italian campaign and John Jordan, an army doctor, received the D.S.O. for performing operations under enemy gunfire on the retreat to Dunkirk.

We had as Director in the Junior Scholasticate Fr H. J. Farrell ('Bertie'), an unusual personality – I understate. He had studied Freud and was practising psychotherapy with beneficial results. Such an attitude was rare in the Catholic Church, especially among priests, at the time. The result was that I learned all about the subconscious at an age when most young people know nothing of such things. I think that Fr Bertie stressed too much the unconscious fear of failure as a factor in psychosomatic illness. But he had remarkable success with certain patients.

We have all been in part educated by what was happening in our immediate world. We were schoolboys in the first years of independent Ireland, but an independent Ireland which still bore the scars of a civil war, and was deeply divided in its political groupings. It was not merely government and opposition in our national parliament: these conventional democratic alignments were overladen with memories of bloodshed, executions, families deprived of breadwinners, children orphaned, all the misery, all the pain, all the unforgiven wounds that are the legacy of fraternal strife.

We did not take conscious account of all this, but it affected our mentality, probably conditioned our attitude to life. But we also had a native Irish government and its activity entered directly into our lives. Under the British administration secondary education had been organised in four grades: preparatory, junior, middle and senior. Each year ended with a public examination, though preparatory had lapsed for some time. The grades were now abolished and two certificates, Intermediate and Leaving, were to replace them. The content of the courses in different subjects was altered. Previously prescribed programmes were limited to carefully selected areas. In particular, English language and literature had comprised certain fixed texts; history was restricted to firmly demarcated periods; languages were also taught with the use of prescribed texts.

Everything was now to be comprehensive. The student was required to have an intelligent understanding of the whole course of European and Irish history. It was no longer 'kings, dates and battles' but, for example, the causes of one or other of the great crises or movements. Instead of a question on one particular prose book, or play, the student would be required to know about the great departments of literature, not, for example, *Macbeth* but 'drama and Shakespeare as a dramatist'.

I was fortunate to have some gifted teachers, especially one of whom I shall write later, Dr McQuaid. I have often stated in public, in homilies at the funeral Masses of cherished lay colleagues, that it is especially the secondary teachers of our country who have made it what it is. Irish boys and girls can compete favourably anywhere with their peers – thanks to our secondary schools. This is not to belittle the contribution of our National Schools or the indispensable need for some of our universities and third level colleges.

Novitiate and University

Before I got into this third level world I had to do my novitiate. I cannot say that I had a perfect rapport with my Novice Master, Fr Evans. I am grateful for the instruction, on traditional lines, imparted by the Novice Master and for the prescribed reading from Rodriguez, which we undertook each day as we walked in procession. A favourite devotion of Fr Evans was to St Joseph, and this I hope I have retained. I made my profession on 1 September 1929. After this I took up my third level studies.

This meant living in the Castle, Blackrock College, a separate building at the time used as a seminary. Our director of Scholastics was Fr John Kearney, a man of strong religious observance, steeped in spirituality; he would later become known as a spiritual writer. I was to attend University College Dublin, and to my delight it would be, by his choice, in the Department of Philosophy, styled at the time Mental and Moral Science. Our Professors were, each in his way, both learned and interesting: Fr John Shine, Logic and Psychology, was abreast of modern developments, though Freud was not mentioned. Fr Denis O'Keefe, Ethics and Political Science, was witty and seasoned his teaching with humour. Mr William Magennis, Metaphysics, the only layman with students entirely clerical; not conventional, highly articulate, known outside the university world as a member of the board for the censorship of books and as a member of the national Senate.

Theological Studies

For my theological studies I was sent to Fribourg, Switzerland, to follow courses at the Dominican university. To live in Switzerland was in itself educational; one learned to appreciate qualities which had ensured a particular ethos, guaranteeing peace and stability. The Irish students who went there in 1934 with me had the great advantage of having a Swiss Superior, Fr Jean Bondallaz, a former African missionary.

We also had living in the house with us a retired Irish missionary bishop, Mgr John O'Gorman, former Vicar Apostolic of Sierra Leone. The French thought very highly of him. I heard the French Provincial say after his death that he had the finest intellect in the entire Congregation. He taught in our French seminary and had given similar service in the US. Despite his immense knowledge and his episcopal dignity we could talk to him as one of ourselves; he lived in an ordinary room on the same corridor as we did. It was inspiring.

At the University we had the good fortune to study under the direction of the great Dominican Order. Our teachers were excellent; in dogmatic and moral theology we followed the *Summa* of St Thomas Aquinas, making direct contact with a great mind – immensely formative. I may single out two professors. Fr François Marie Braun, professor of the New Testament, came of a Belgian family with strong links with Dom Columba Marmion; he had been a lawyer, and had the Irish Benedictine as his spiritual director and his hero. He would later be chaplain to the exiled king of his country, spiritual director to Baudoin and Fabiola. The other professor whom I got to know well was the director of my doctorate dissertation, Fr Benoit Lavaud, a méri-odonal.

Fr Lavaud had been a captain in the French army in the First World War – priests are not exempt from conscription. I think that Fr Lavaud had some sympathy with *L'Action française*. I am sure he had accepted Rome's ruling, though I gathered that it was without enthusiasm. He was well-known as a writer and was in the Maritain circle, not perhaps in the innermost sector.

We met occasionally and he talked encouragingly with me about the subject of my thesis, *Ven Francis Libermann and Spiritual Direction*. We also had time to discuss other matters. My mentor told me about his war experience, one incident amusing. The colonel in the officer's mess knew, as did the others, that he was a priest. The colonel was anti-clerical and missed few opportunities of giving the priest captain pointed jabs. One day he went too far. The subject of conversation was women. Captain Lavaud knew that his senior officer had a weakness in that area. So when he came out with the customary ritual criticism about the church as the enemy of women, the time was right for a sharp retort: 'Eh, colonel, you know if I was a woman, I think I'd feel safer with the church than with you.' A hasty departure; cheers almost from the other officers and no more anti-clerical talk.

Those years in Fribourg were immediately pre-war. We were increasingly conscious of Hitler, would occasionally hear his raucous voice on the radio. I still see as if it were yesterday, the glaring poster that met us on our way to the University, *Le coup de force rhénan*, the morning after the invasion of the Rhineland. The danger of a challenge to him passed. Then came Munich. I remember listening to the broadcast voice of Pius XI as he welcomed the momentary peace; he spoke of the 'meek St Wenceslaus'.

Reflecting on my education

I was a student in two universities in the pre-conciliar age and have to thank God that he brought me into a religious congregation which would be so generous to me. Not only have I no reproach to make to the educational system within which I was formed, I still feel sentiments of admiration and of gratitude when I look back on those years.

Education is a complex process, given cohesion and unity by the sense of a commanding ideal, by an educator of genius, even, though rarely, by a fellow student with charismatic power. My great blessing was, in Dublin and in Fribourg, to gain a deep sense of the faith and of the universality of the church, existentially, as I had conviction on these truths already.

There is no substitute for experience. Venerable Francis Libermann held that it did not even come with holiness or great learning. I benefited by it in my education. In University College Dublin I saw by experience what the priesthood meant to my peers, how expert knowledge in the philosophical sciences could go along with the faith. In Fribourg I learned, again by experience, how deliberate choice of the priestly vocation was wholehearted and efficacious in young men coming from ethnic and national backgrounds widely different from mine.

It has been said that the real test of education is the power it gives to grow in self-education. It must also occasionally stand the test of assisting others in the same process.

Educating others

I had some experience of attempting to educate others in the prefecting system, which I think our Congregation borrowed from the Jesuits. Half way through the seminary course, we were sent to the colleges to help in teaching and in day to day running of the school, supervising pupils in recreation and in study time, organising games, and participating, if we felt like it. I did so in Rockwell, playing with the house team, and in St Mary's, playing with the past students' team. Prefecting was an ideal system of training, and it was good for recruitment to the Congregation.

It all meant that when I returned to Blackrock in 1939 I was not entering an unknown world. I had asked to be sent on the missions, on three separate occasions. I had even torn up, shortly before leaving Fribourg, notes on English literature which I had made in Rockwell and kept, but now thought useless. I was at once given an English literature class and sorely regretted what I had done. The decision to send me to Blackrock was taken by a priest to whom I am deeply indebted. He had taught me in Blackrock College, he was my dean in Rockwell when I was prefecting there, and now he was my Provincial, the one who had sent me to Fribourg where he had studied himself. He was Fr Daniel Murphy, 'Dr Dan', a Kerryman with prodigious mental energy, and noted for his attention to detail.

So I set to work, for this was the will of God. My dean was a fellow Limerick man, Fr Con Daly. I was fortunate in my pupils, many of whom have remained lifelong friends.

At times I found the drudgery of the classroom, and ancillary tasks such as correcting written work and tests, very trying. I was trained in philosophy and theology and here I was at times telling boys how to spell in French the equivalent of 'cat and dog'. If people asked me why I kept on, I had this answer which may appear complacent: 'A better man than me spent his working years cutting and hammering bits of wood, and see where he is now!' But what really kept me going was the quality of the boys I had to deal with, and the friends whom God gave me. All of which is related to the special ethos and character of Blackrock College.

I was blessed that I did not have to use corporal punishment. It was not allowed to teachers in the college. Only the Dean of

Studies could administer it. There was a golden rule in my class: no one could with impunity laugh – in a mocking manner – at another boy, and I was particularly severe if the victim was in any way disadvantaged or vulnerable. I would stop the class if this happened, call on the offender to listen carefully and then threaten him with dire effects if he ever did this again. He never did; nor did he resent my warning, for he knew that if he was the victim I would be on his side. It was a way of teaching boys that they must respect one another.

Teaching Religious Knowledge

Religious knowledge has not been an easy subject in the curriculum. To illustrate that assertion one would need to discuss the whole problem of catechetics, and trace the history of training centres in different countries. I shall stay with my own experience. It is limited to second level students. In that sector we had for years a text book entitled *Apologetics and Christian Doctrine,* the work of a former Maynooth professor who was for a while Coadjutor Archbishop of Sydney, Michael Sheahan. His books were used in the final years of secondary studies where I was operating. All was well and my pupils were as satisfied with the contents, as I had been when I was their age. Then came the crisis of the sixties. Why it came is not yet clear. A sequel to Vatican II? This would scarcely be a sustainable thesis. 'Fall-out' in the classroom from the explosion in the college campuses of the US, or the Paris revolution when a handful of students almost toppled De Gaulle?

Young people everywhere were affected. I recall passing through Rome and hearing from my former classmate, Fr Anthony Hampson, then Director of Scholastics in our seminary there, stories of unrest and even defiance of his authority. The prestigious Gregorian University did not escape the epidemic. Fr Hampson had come back to our teaching staff and one day I met him coming out of a Religious Knowledge class. 'Michael,' he exclaimed 'this is worse than Rome.' That was saying a lot! Remember that the boys were from staunch Catholic families, whose brothers in some cases would have been with us with no speck of dissent.

It wasn't so much dissent, as an urge, I almost said an itch, to question everything. The questioning was often accompanied by lack of reverence – an understatement. It was going so far that one day one of our most experienced educationalists, Fr Michael McCarthy, raised with me the advisability of continuing with Religious Knowledge as a part of the curriculum. We held on.

Then suddenly the storm abated and died down. This too is not easy to explain. For me there were two telling moments. I recall going into a Religious Knowledge class and hearing a boy ask me: 'Father, will you explain to us the meaning of faith?' He could not know how astonished and delighted I was, especially as he seemed utterly indifferent to what his peers in the classroom would think. Then I was overjoyed when another boy asked me if I intended to show them the slides on the Shroud of Turin. Yes, I replied. A few days later he said to me rather plaintively: 'You promised us the slides on the Shroud. When will we see them?' I reassured him. The slides had been made by an expert, Dr Alfred O'Rahilly, who was living with us in the college.

I was on the state register of secondary teachers and entitled to a pension from the year 1976, when I was sixty-five years of age. I ceased to teach secular subjects but continued with Religious Knowledge for ten years. Then I thought it was time to go, as I had demands of many kinds to meet. I live among the boys in the Castle and retain my admiration for them; many of the families are known to me through representatives of previous generations. It is another reminder to me of all I owe Blackrock College; it explains the dedication of this book.

2. Priesthood and Priests

The question of my vocation concerns myself personally. How did I get this amazing gift of God? The one wishing to be a priest had to convince an ecclesiastical authority, bishop or religious superior, that his interior urge, his sense of a 'call', was valid. Then they issued the legal call. He was accepted and trained for the office. In the twenties of the present century, a French theologian, Fr Lahitton, had examined the whole question of the call with drastic results. He contended that the real call was from the church authority. The candidate presented himself. If he was accepted he had the call, the vocation. Not everyone was in agreement.

My sense of the call was expressed in unusual circumstances. A parish priest of Newcastle West, Fr Hallinan, was know to my mother. He was appointed Bishop of Limerick. On his first visit to his former parish, the family met him for a brief moment. He asked me what I was going to be – I was about ten years of age. To the astonishment of my parents I replied: 'A Holy Ghost Father.' When the opportunity came I went to Blackrock College, where I received the education which I have described.

I had a priestly presence about me wherever I was thereafter, in Ireland and in Switzerland. I may interject the remark that this did not at any time inhibit understanding of the laity; it may have facilitated it. I have also noted that when I have spoken to audiences about the mysterious dignity of the priestly office, it is lay people who have been most appreciative, urging me to go on talking like that.

I was preparing for the priesthood. Yet the overwhelming emphasis in all my training was on the religious life. Why was this? I was not to get the answer to that question at any time up to my ordination. I spent three years in Fribourg before this most important event, two after it. I have racked my memory to discover if I heard one single lecture on the priesthood in the entire course of my training.

For the moment this is not a criticism or a value judgement, but a statement of fact. It certainly invites reflection. In a society where members were both priests and religious, the tendency was to focus attention on the duties of the religious life. If this preference belittled the priestly vocation it would be wholly unjustified. Religious life is a state instituted by men, organised by men, and subject to decisions by men. It is approved and blessed by the church as a form of dedicated life. But it has not an intrinsic, unchangeable divine guarantee.

This the priesthood certainly has. The priesthood adds to the divinisation of the soul effected by baptism and confirmation a further dimension, a more profound configuration to the priesthood of Christ himself. The priestly character imprinted on the soul cannot be effaced. When one is released from the vows of the religious state, one is freed from every quality which it implies. Once a priest always a priest. No power on earth or in heaven can remove the priestly character. This is a mystery undoubtedly. But it seems to me that it is a mystery on which we must reflect more and more. I would not like to discuss whether failure to do this has something to do with the decline in the number of priestly vocations in recent times.

The one person who showed a practical interest in my priesthood was an English woman who came to live in Dublin, an invalid when I met her, Mrs A. F. E. Partridge. She had the power to help priests. She had written a book which I helped to publish, *The Priests' Crusade*. It was an attempt to stir idealism in the sacerdotal body: valiant, wise yet very readable.

Work for a priest?

I had a problem with some of the work I was given. I had a difficulty in relating secondary school classes to the priesthood.

But I was under obedience, and that was that. I had been refused for the missions, and I was likewise refused when I offered my services as a military chaplain during the second world war. Would I have made a good missionary? Or a good military chaplain?

Obedience came to my rescue. Our Provincial, Dr Daniel Murphy, assigned me, as he did others, to preach retreats to nuns during the summer vacation. These retreats were lengthy, eight full days. In the classroom I had in Religious Knowledge another essentially priestly task – which does not mean that it cannot be done by lay people.

With time, priestly work of different kinds came my way. One evening a stalwart of the Legion of Mary, Jock McGallogly, came to the college and asked to see me. Would I become a Spiritual Director to his praesidium, *Mater Salvatoris*? I accepted the invitation and am grateful to Jock. He had an interesting personal history, I learned afterwards. He had come over from Glasgow at the age of sixteen to take part in the 1916 Easter Rising. He later described wittily, for the Bureau of Military History, how he and his fellow insurgents, led by the poet and idealist Joseph Mary Plunket, boarded a tram in Terenure to reach their action post, the only army to go into battle in a tram! Taken captive, he suffered imprisonment for years. He was tough, direct and totally free from bitterness; an excellent Legionary of Mary, and my tutor, whom I remember with much gratitude.

I also had pastoral duty as chaplain to the college troop of scouts; it was the first established in a secondary school, and despite some initial scepticism lasted very well. After my tenure of office, the troop went from strength to strength, some of its members achieving office at national level.

I also, as I narrate elsewhere, took up writing on religious subjects; if I did not fully inform it with priestly motivation, then I shall have to answer to the Almighty. Writing reminds me of a big problem in a priest's life: how to harness his energy to supernatural work and eschew personal ambition. Many writers are tempted to vanity; to deny the possibility would be foolish.

What is the solution? Wait until one's intention is wholly pure? Then who will write and when? I am borrowing the remark made by St Francis de Sales to his sister, who said: 'Francis, you preach beautifully. Do you practise it?' His reply, 'In that case who will preach?' One must keep on, trusting in God to purify one's motives.

Priests and the Second Vatican Council

As I was commenting on the Second Vatian Council week by week in the *Catholic Standard*, and in a more general way in *The Leader*, I was obliged to follow the debates in Rome. During the first three sessions, 1962-1964, there was nothing much to report on the priesthood. Up to the fourth session it looked as if the assembly in Rome would not make much advance on what is contained in one article of the Constitution on the Church. There priests are seen very much in close relationship with bishops: they 'depend on the bishops in the exercises of their own proper power, they are prudent co-operators of the episcopal college and its support and mouthpiece ... they have a sharing in the priesthood and mission of the bishop'.

Père (later Cardinal) Congar OP reported that a French priest who was asked if he was interested in the Council replied: 'I'm not a bishop, a layman or a separated brother; they're not interested in me in Rome.' The sequel to Vatican II was to show that this was a serious issue. The Constitution on the Church devoted eight articles to bishops, with this sentence which again seems to minimise the role of priests: 'In the person of bishops then, to whom the priests render assistance, the Lord Jesus Christ supreme high priest, is present in the midst of the faithful.' I note that one of those who eventually secured commendable teaching on priesthood was a member of our Congregation, Fr Joseph Lécuyer, in his own right a theologian of the sacred calling.

Fr Lécuyer helped rescue the conciliar text from a paltry state. It was proposed to offer to the priests of the church a set of twelve propositions, to some extent platitudinous. Would this have been due recognition of the immense services of priests to the Catholic Church? They have given the witness of blood – the Polish martyrology alone carries the names of 3,000 priests; their work on the missions stirred the admiration of Pius XI, for here they have been almost entirely pioneers; their contribution to Catholic education at every level has been incalculable; they provided the new theological insights which were the very substance of conciliar thinking; to the Council they provided the experts on whom the bishops depended.

In the fourth session of this great assembly there was a sudden awakening to a simple truth: whatever an army without a general can do, a general without an army can do nothing. Bishops without priests would be in this situation. They gave evidence of their anxiety, which was almost panic. When, on official orders, a full text was submitted on *The Life and Ministry of Priests*, the bishops really set to work. On the proposed draft they submitted additions or amendments which ran to 330 large pages of *Acta Synodalia* (the official record). They were later allowed to put forward *Modi*, precise verbal amendments to the final text. Here they exceeded anything seen in the entire history of Vatican II: 5,400.

Was it too late? Despite the excellence of the decree, was there something, by way of effect, of what the French priest had said? Is there some truth in the view, or hope, sometimes expressed, that the next General Council will have as one of its main themes, the priesthood?

Fr Edward Leen

Fr Leen was the first priest writer with whom I came in contact. He was first Dean of Studies, then President, of Blackrock College when I came there as a boy, remaining four and a half years. He constituted with Fr McQuaid, Fr Farrell and Fr Heelan a group that infused idealism into the system within which we were formed. I did not have much contact with him beyond listening to the occasional talks he gave us as president, and following his religious knowledge class in my last year.

When I returned to the college as a seminarian after my novitiate, I was before long overjoyed to know that he had ceased to be president and would be on the teaching staff with us. We felt that his abrupt departure from the presidential office had not been without hurt. He was now becoming known as a lecturer, retreat giver, would soon be known to a wider audience as a spiritual writer. His image had in it something of the heroic, the utterly single-minded.

Fr Leen lectured in psychology and cosmology. I did not follow his courses as I was a student at University College. But I fell within his radiance and he consented to become my spiritual director.

When I was leaving the scholasticate, i.e. the seminary, to do prefecting, I went to him for advice. I was surprised at what this uncompromising spiritual teacher said to me. It was something like this: 'The prefects of former times knew how to deal with the boys, but were not obviously pious; those nowadays, I'm told, are very pious but can't deal with the boys. I'd prefer the former type.' At first surprised, I saw on reflection what he meant. I can also say that those with whom I did my prefecting knew how to handle the boys, to impose discipline while remaining friendly.

I learned later that Fr Leen had been a prefect in Rockwell College, and had played with the Rockwell house team at the level of Munster Senior Rugby. I was told, I hope reliably, that on one occasion, his opponent was a legendary figure in Irish rugby and in world war one, Basil McClear, an Irish international, captain in his regiment, dying heroically – on this my uncle, who served in his regiment, was my witness.

I lost direct contact with Fr Leen, but followed his career with interest and pride. When he submitted a first book for publication, *Progress through Mental Prayer*, it was turned down by two firms, one of them Irish. He was then fortunate to meet the great Catholic publisher, Frank Sheed. He had confessed some time before to a friend that waiting for the final decision was a very great strain on his nerves. It was not only the expectancy of an author about the success or failure of a first book. He felt, rightly or wrongly, that his name aroused opposition in certain quarters. An article which he published on the Mass, in the *Irish Ecclesiastical Record*, the church establishment organ at the time, had been censured by Irish bishops.

Divine Providence, as events worked out, put him largely beyond the danger. His works reached Ireland after they had been read, approved, published and praised abroad. Apparently the decisive word in the choice by Sheed and Ward was Maisie Ward, to whom her husband gave the manuscript.

Progress through Mental Prayer appeared in the autumn of 1935. It was received with respect and eulogy in Catholic reviews and periodicals and in the literary pages of the press. Its impact on the Catholic reading public was distinctive. Religious communities in England and Ireland took it up as a book with a special message. When a little later it was published in the United States the enthusiasm was still greater. There was a vital pulse all through the book. This was what drew people to the book, the living quality emanating from it.

Readers felt the same attraction in Fr Leen's second work, *In the Likeness of Christ*, which came out the following year. It was a substantial work. Some surprise was caused by its rapid appearance, but Fr Leen had a considerable quantity of manuscript material accumulated, and was far ahead of the publisher. He also provided the clear affirmative answer to those who asked: 'Can Fr Leen maintain the standard of his first work?' He surpassed it. *In the Likeness of Christ* excels *Progress through Mental Prayer* not only in measure and scope, but in its spiritual perception and its synthesis of high Christian wisdom.

One year after the appearance of *In the Likeness of Christ, The Holy Ghost* was published. 'The work,' wrote Fr Leen in the preface, 'has been prompted by a desire to popularise the wonders of Catholic theology and to give the ordinary readers a working knowledge of the divine life imparted by the Holy Ghost to the souls of the just.' Not many Catholics were, at that time, writing on the Holy Spirit. The author went on to publish *Why the Cross* and *The True Vine and its Branches. Why the Cross* is probably his best work. He wrote it from deep reflection on the Passion of Christ and from his own experience. Though he wrote, 'The Cross of Christ is a veritable theory of life', he fully justified Christian joy and happiness.

Fr Leen wrote during or after his American tour *The Church before Pilate* and shortly before his death *What is Education?*, based on studies he had consigned to writing over the years. As he stated, it is the answer of Christian humanism to the question title.

In his last years he was much in demand as a lecturer. Two lectures which he gave attracted more than usual attention. One was to the Institute of Architects. The other was surrounded with controversy. The Friends of the National Collections, patrons of the arts, had purchased for a Dublin gallery a portrait of the dead Christ by Rouault. There was opposition to its acceptance, so a public debate was arranged. Fr Leen's talk defending the work of Rouault was very impressive. The decision to reject it was not rescinded. Instead it was presented to Maynooth College. It was doubtless his aesthetic outlook which prompted the distinguished painter, Mainie Jellett, close friend of Evie Hone, to ask him to assist her in preparing for death. She was a member of the Church of Ireland.

An important factor in Fr Leen's work among all classes, especially the highly cultured, was his evident intellectual power. Academically it won him the gold medal for excellence in the Gregorian University and enabled him in a post-graduate dissertation, presented at University College Dublin, to challenge a sacred tenet of his professor.

But intellect, to carry effective conviction in religious matters, does best when it is clothed with experience. This came to Fr Leen though collaboration with a great missionary, Bishop Joseph Shanahan. As a boy in Rockwell he had come under the influence of Fr Shanahan, then on the college staff. Later he served for a while with him on the missionfield in Nigeria. He especially supported the religious foundation made by the

Bishop, the Missionary Sisters of the Holy Rosary, initially based in Killeshandra, Co Cavan. After the death of his friend on Christmas Day 1943, he contributed an important article to the review *Studies* on the great missionary career. Bishop Shanahan was directly linked with St Patrick's Missionary Society, for the founding members had been volunteers in his jurisdiction. The foundress of the Medical Missionaries of Mary, Mother Mary Martin, had also worked there as a volunteer. There was something majestic about Bishop Shanahan; people often stopped just to look at him.

My last personal meeting with his priest friend was following the retreat which he preached to the priests of the Irish Province in the summer of 1944. I talked to him after it and was overjoyed to hear him speak with such conviction about Our Lady. 'Devotion to her is a grace,' he said. As I knew from my brother Fr Pat, he had had a problem with the growing devotion to her, this because his thinking was so profoundly Christo-centric. A change had come, for he dedicated his last work, on education, to the Immaculate Heart of Mary. After his death, papers written by him over the years were published with some papers by his friend, Fr Kearney, under the title, *Our Blessed Lady*. Was the change due to the friendship with Frank Duff, especially as they had suffered together? Such a question is not to suggest that Fr Leen lacked traditional Catholic devotion to the Mother of God. He was to realise that there was no danger in the increasing piety he saw. One is reminded of the people who went to St Pius X at the beginning of the century when Lourdes was drawing ever larger crowds; they feared that Christ would be displaced. 'Not at all,' said the Pope, 'the Son will be seen to work miracles at the prayer of the Mother.' How often it is when the Blessed Sacrament passes that the miracles occur. How wonderful is the liturgical and personal honour given to the Eucharist there and at so many other Marian shrines.

Fr Leen knew early in November of 1944 that he would die soon. He used to say that he had no fear of death – he once said to a nun who questioned him on the point: 'Less fear than if I had to talk to you people.' He did say to my brother, Fr Pat: 'It is different when you know that the bell has rung – that eternity is upon you.' He went to Killeshandra for a final visit, bidding farewell to Mother Brigid, his very dear friend since the days when they worked together in Nigeria. She was Superior General of the congregation. He asked her if he were not buried in Kimmage would they bury him in Killeshandra – he did not wish to go to Deansgrange. He was buried in Kimmage.

He returned to Kimmage, said goodbye to a friend and colleague, Fr Bernard Fennelly with the words: 'He has given me great peace.' My brother accompanied him in the taxi to the Mater Hospital where he would have tests. He confided that he was happy the way certain important questions where he had responsibility had been solved. The tests in the Mater seemed to indicate that, from a health point of view, things were well. The day after he got this word, he collapsed in his room; twenty-four hours later he was dead, 10 November 1944. He had offered himself as a victim to God; the oblation was now sealed forever. His status in Catholic Ireland was manifest in the numerous messages of sympathy received in Kimmage and in the attendance at his funeral; dignitaries of Church and State honoured him, as did representatives of many religious congregations. For myself, as for many others who saw him as a luminary of God, it was an immensely poignant moment. I regard him as a saint.

Fr Daniel Brottier

I turn to one who will undoubtedly be so proclaimed officially, a French member of our congregation, Blessed Daniel Brottier. During my student days in Fribourg, Père Brottier, director of the *Orphelins Apprentis* of Auteuil, came to spend his holidays in a house of the Congregation across the road from ours. He came to lunch with us one day and afterwards we sat around under some trees in the garden chatting. He was delightful, and told us about a visit he had paid the previous day to the Carthusian monastery nearby, the Val Sainte. He teased one of the fathers over some difficulty he had with a local bishop, not the bishop of our diocese. One day I met him personally and he entrusted me with a letter for our superior.

Not very long afterwards we heard the news of his death, on 28 February 1936. I felt the urge to know more about him. What I learned is a rather exceptional story. Père Brottier, after being ordained for a French diocese, chose to enter our Congregation. He was sent as a missionary, his great hope, to Senegal. Here he became friendly with a great missionary bishop, Mgr Hyacinthe Jalabert. Ill-health forced him to return to France. The first world war had broken out. He was of military age but was exempt on health grounds. He enrolled as a chaplain and served throughout the entire period of hostilities.

Since he had been again and again in mortal danger, with close comrades dying around him, especially during the battle of Verdun which took hundreds of thousands of casualties, one thing completely perplexed him. How and why did he survive? When the war was over he got the answer. Mgr Jalabert was back in France and when Père Brottier put this question to him, he opened his breviary and showed his friend his photo; on the reverse side was a picture of Sister Thérèse of Lisieux – she had not yet been beatified. 'Every day I prayed to her to bring you back safe.'

A decisive moment. The ex-chaplain vowed in the depth of his soul that he would show his gratitude to his heavenly intercessor. Before long he had his opportunity. Mgr le Roy, Superior General, summoned him and informed him that the Archbishop of Paris had asked the congregation to take over a Paris Boys' Orphanage. It was situated in the fashionable district of Auteuil, and at that time one could say that it had known better days.

He did not forget his promise to Blessed Thérèse, as she now was. He decided to build a church in her honour in the grounds of the orphanage. For this, permission was needed from the Archbishop of Paris. An appointment was fixed and the good father asked his heavenly protectress to give him a sign of her involvement: nine thousand francs before he met the Archbishop.

Nothing happened. But the appointment must be kept. A taxi

came to take the priest to his destination. Then one of these people who have a special skill in halting you as you have not a minute to spare, arrived on the scene. 'Père Brottier, I want to speak to you.' 'Mme, you can see the taxi waiting; I have an appointment with the Archbishop of Paris in a quarter hour's time.' 'Father, I only want to give you an offering for your work.' 'It must be nine thousand francs.' It was ten thousand. Thus began a chain of magic happenings. Every day while the construction of the church was in progress, a thousand franc note would somewhere or other reach Père Brottier. Just reassurance from on high.

The church was the first built in honour of the saint – she was canonised in 1925. It became the Paris centre of devotion in her honour, with special ceremonies annually on her feast day. But with her help, Père Brottier did wonders in Auteuil. When he took over it was an orphanage. Under his direction it became 'The Apprentice Orphans' (*Les Orphelins Apprentis*). He provided expert training for the young boys and soon they were producing high quality goods of every kind, from chocolate to radio sets. When Cardinal Pacelli visited Paris he needed to replenish his failing stock of personal cards. Auteuil was recommended to him.

Numbers increased: at Père Brottier's take-over there were one hundred and fifty. At his death there were one thousand three hundred, based on Auteuil and other centres; some were benefiting by his scheme to allow boys agricultural initiation, *Le Foyer rural*.

All the time the good priest was faithful to his first love, the missionfield of Senegal. Mgr Jalabert had appointed him his representative in France, chiefly as fund-raiser for a gigantic project, the erection in the city of Dakar of a cathedral which would be a memorial to all Frenchmen and women who had died in Africa.

This commission became sacred for Père Brottier after a great missionary tragedy. Mgr Jalabert, with several missionaries on their way back to Africa, was caught in a shipwreck. All died and little was salvaged. One item did survive, the breviary within which he had kept the picture of St Thérèse with Père Brottier's photo. It can be seen in the museum at Auteuil. Another coincidence I record. A devout Senegalese at the time of the shipwreck had just had a baby son. In memory of Mgr Hyacinthe Jalabert he named his child Hyacinthe. Today that child is the Cardinal Archbishop of Dakar, Hyacinthe Thiandoum.

The cathedral at Dakar is named 'Le Souvenir Africain'. On the facade is the motto: Grateful France to her glorious dead (*A ses morts glorieux la France reconnaissante*). For the inaugural blessing on 2 February 1936, Cardinal Verdier was the Papal Legate. Père Brottier could not make the journey. He had ensured the reality. Asked about this time how much he had collected for all his charities, he replied 'twenty-five million francs'.

He died on 28 February 1936. Immediately things began to happen. I heard a good deal about this first-hand from his collaborator and his first biographer, Père Pichon. I asked him if he thought that Père Brottier, beside whom he had worked for years, was a saint. No, not until the day of his death. He had thought him a fine man, with immense ability and capacity for work. But when he died, with just a mere word on the radio, the church at Auteuil was invaded. So many people came to do him honour, to pray to him, that the carpet in front of the altar was worn.

People began to report miraculous healings, help of different kinds. Père Pichon himself told me about an amusing heavenly sign. He was, some days after the funeral, totting up the expenses. It came to eighty-four thousand francs. Just then a lady entered his office and handed him a sum of exactly eighty-four thousand francs.

It became clear that the man who had so honoured the saint of Lisieux would himself one day be officially declared a saint by the church. The process of beatification was quickly opened. Miracles were abundant which, as well as meeting a canonical requirement, was a stimulus to keep on with the work. Certain aspects of Père Brottier's career which may have prompted criticism during his life were now a recommendation – such as his use of the cinema, frowned upon by some Catholic authorities until the Pope urged the faithful to use it for the apostolate.

All was ready for the first phase in glorification of the good father of orphans, the heroic chaplain, advocate among ex-soldiers and chaplain of national unity 'as at the front'. His life had been intertwined with Carmel and it was fitting that a young Carmelite, Sister Elizabeth of the Trinity, of the Carmel of Dijon, should be beatified with him in 1984. He had once been a welcome visitor to the homeland of the Pope.

3. Writing

The Catholic Standard

The Catholic Standard had been attached to the diocese of Dublin but was now being run by a board which had representatives of the main political parties. I began by writing a weekly column for the editor, Michael McDonagh, a man who had come to the paper with experience as a Reuter correspondent in the Far East. A crisis occurred when Michael withdrew. I happened to be in the office when the board met to appoint his successor. I was more than surprised when the chairman, Patrick Baxter of the Farmers' party, came from the boardroom and asked me if I would make a partnership with a staff member, Peter Kilroy, whom they would then appoint editor. I was to do the editorials. I agreed. So for fourteen years I wrote every editorial that appeared in the paper. I missed one week, only because my copy which had been sent in, went astray. Sometimes we had two editorials.

I was fortunate in my editor and, in the years through which we worked together, Peter was conspicuous for a quality which we are all ready to preach to others, but which is not too easy to practise, humility. In our joint work we achieved a harmony which I look back on with utter joy. I was ready to meet any request from him, which meant that I would do a piece on anything that was of interest to Catholic readers, unsigned naturally. I think that it is bad to have the same signature more than once in a paper. All the time I had the sense of complete freedom in the choice of themes for the leading articles.

All this began in 1957. Soon we were to be witnesses of one major event after another in the Catholic Church. The long career of Pius XII came to an end, leaving a sense of emptiness which few who were not then living can imagine. Then came his unknown successor, John XXIII. Unknown but not for long. He summoned the Council and lived to see its first session completed. I am not here attempting, even briefly, to deal with the history of the Council. I merely record that in a Catholic paper the demand for copy was larger and more insistent.

I could not go to Rome as many journalists did. I had to rely on news agency reports which, after the first session, were ample. It was the NCWC service that we used. As the sessions went on, I found myself typing several columns of material week by week. It was laborious, but highly enjoyable.

The Leader

The problem was time. For most of a year before I began to write so much for the *Catholic Standard*, I had a similar commitment to *The Leader*. I had been writing feature articles for this fortnightly for some time. I think I may have been invited to do so by the editor, Nuala Moran, daughter of the founder and first editor, D. P. Moran. I met her at functions of the Legion of Mary. Nuala was continuing the paper out of respect for her father's memory. In 1956 she was looking for an editorial writer. I think she may have suggested that I try my hand. I may have made the offer myself. She was a courageous lady, with whom it was an honour to collaborate.

The Leader was an opinion periodical, independent. When I undertook to supply so much copy it had just begun to recover from a libel action which had been the talk of the town. Patrick Kavanagh, a distinguished poet, one of Dublin's celebrity set as only Dublin can have them, had sued the paper over a profile of him which had appeared anonymously. The clash between Patrick and Mr John A. Costello, SC (one-time Taoiseach) filled columns of the *Irish Times* and no doubt stimulated conversation in the cultural haunts of the city. *The Leader* won the action, but a new trial was ordered by the appeal court. Both sides agreed to make an out-of-court settlement. To Nuala Moran's honour she never divulged to me the name of the author who cost her so much. She merely told me that a number of barristers had read the manuscript before it was printed and passed it.

On the international scene there were large-scale events to report and judge. At home we followed a line that would then be called liberal, calling for enlargement of the social services, free education to the level of the pupil's ability. I thought that opposition to help of the kind on *a priori* grounds was unjustifiable; it could mean the well-off, including the clergy, telling the poor that it was good for their moral fibre to remain disadvantaged. Highly intelligent people dreaded 'statism', possibly because they saw no other form than Marxist regimes.

About that time I appeared on the same university platform as Noel Browne, and told him that many Catholics would support him if he approached them sympathetically. Some bishops had opposed his 'Mother and Child' scheme on bad advice; they thought it wrong to have a free state service. Noel drove me home and until 1 o'clock in the morning we discussed the whole thing. I was deeply touched some years ago when through Michael Gill, publisher of his autobiography, he sent me his love – his exact word; he thought that I had eased his conscience. Just at the moment of crisis I met a seminary rector, a future bishop. He reminded me that there was a free Health Service in the Vatican!

In *The Leader* we dealt with the conciliar issue of religious liberty without fear of the abuses some people anticipated. I had for a long time seen the fallacy of 'error has no rights'; rights inhere in persons and persons in error have rights. We supported the idea of a united Europe, not that we thought that it would mean paradise on earth. In a local context, we supported Limerick's claim to a university.

Other Periodicals and Journals

I had contributed articles singly or in series to a number of periodicals – the *Blackrock College Annual*, which I edited for two years, and the *Missionary Annals* of our province, domestic organs, the *Irish Rosary*, a Dominican publication. The first pamphlet I wrote was *The Secret of Knock*; it was followed by a number of others. Later, much later, I sent articles, which were accepted, to the editors of theological reviews, *The Pastoral and Homiletic Review* and the *Irish Ecclesiastical Record*. I contributed from time to time to the *Knock Shrine Annual*, prompted in this by admiration for the unique apparition, and my deep sense of gratitude to Mr Justice Coyne and his wife, Judy. In passing I note that she, as editor of this publication for fifty-eight years, may have a world record.

Golden Eagle Books

My first venture in book publishing was a short work on Our Lady, *This Age and Mary*, in 1947. I had also written a work on St Joseph, entitled *The King Uncrowned*. Though steeped in journalism I did not give up writing books. I decided to enlarge my book on Our Lady and I had a publisher at my doorstep. The *Catholic Standard* decided to launch a publishing company. It was called Golden Eagle Books. I was invited to join the board which meant, to my great joy, making a closer acquaintance with two writers whom I knew and valued very highly, Robert Farren and Francis McManus, also board members. The venture did not last very long, but it gave me a little understanding of book production from the side of the one who must carry the financial risk. The board accepted my book entitled *Mediatress of All Graces*, and I secured for them the translation rights of Fr Reginald Garrigou-Lagrange's *Mother of the Saviour*, the English rendering from the gifted pen of my religious colleague, former classmate, Fr Bernard Kelly, C.S.Sp.

A book which I planned from the writings of Hilaire Belloc was turned down. Eleanor Jebb, the great man's daughter, came to see me about this time and assured me that her father would welcome the project, if it were feasible. I had in mind a collection of all the passages in his vast corpus (about one hundred and fifty volumes) dealing with Ireland. A principal item would be the chapter on the Irish Famine in his short history of England. Mrs Jebb told me that her father wondered if there would be enough material for a book. I thought so and still think so and if any enterprising reader of these lines wishes to undertake the compilation I shall be delighted to help him or her.

It is not a digression from my main theme in this chapter to mention that Belloc had an Irish grandmother, Louise Swanton, daughter of Colonel Swanton of the Irish brigade in the French army: she had taken him as a child to the spot where as a child she had seen the assault on the Bastille during the French Revolution – Belloc's books on the Revolution would fascinate me. As a schoolboy I heard him lecture twice, in Blackrock College on *The Conspiracy against Christendom*, and in a Dublin theatre on *Anti-Catholic History*. I pray that he will return, as his friend G. K. Chesterton has come back. What we, of that generation, owe them!

St Joseph

I am one of those who believe that St Joseph has been neglected in the Catholic Church, which owes so much to him. Evidence of this is the boycott of him imposed on the Second Vatican Council by certain progressive theologians among the experts. He is not mentioned in 100,000 words of the Council documents save in a quotation from Eucharistic Prayer I, the old Roman Canon. There is here a double irony. John XXIII had declared the saint protector of the Council, issuing a splendid letter to justify his decision; the same Pope inserted his name in the Roman Canon.

The second irony is more painful. The silence on the saint was meant to appease Protestants. Interviewed about that time the greatest Protestant theologian of modern times, Karl Barth, was asked if he had reservations about St Joseph, as he was known to have about Our Lady. 'I love St Joseph.' was his reply. 'I rejoiced when John XXIII put his name in the Canon. I shall ask Pope Paul VI to bring him into prominence. He protected the Child; he will protect the Church.' Still more severe was the criticism of the Council for the omission by the Swiss Calvinist professor at Neuchatel University, J. J. von Allmen.

I decided to bring out a second book on the saint, who, I am convinced, will have a decisive role in the future of the church. My methodology was as yet imperfect, but I got considerable assistance from Michael Gill, my publisher, of the well-known Dublin firm Gill and Macmillan. The book on Pius XII, about which I shall write later, I decided to bring out on my own; the second edition was taken by Four Courts Press.

Dictionnaire de Spiritualité

The Croatian president of the Pontifical Marian Academy, Fr Karl Ballic OFM, gave me the honour of presenting the opening paper at the 1975 International Mariological Congress held in Rome. Among those present was Fr Rayez SJ, one of the editorial staff of the *Dictionnaire de Spiritualité*. He invited me, there and then, to do the article on the *Lorica*, St Patrick's Breastplate, for their encyclopedic work. Later, in their house in Chantilly, he provided me with the documentation. This house, *Les Fontaines*, has one of the finest theological libraries in Europe. It had been a Jesuit seminary; now, since there are no seminarists, it is a *Centre Culturel*.

When Fr Rayez died I began the same happy relationship with his successor, Fr André Derville, who has an unbounded capacity for work. The *Dictionnaire de Spiritualité* has been edited and published from Chantilly. It is now complete. Altogether I contributed twenty seven articles to the work, which stands as a superb monument of scholarship.

My articles included Pius XII and St Patrick. The latter I was slow to undertake. There has been much controversy recently about our national saint. I was able to do some research in the library of the Bollandistes in Brussels. Here, in an excellent file placed at my disposal by the devoted librarian, Fr Cerckel SJ, I found valuable material from Fr Paul Grosjean, the Bollandiste specialist on Irish hagiography.

I composed my article and sent the first draft to Bishop Hanson in Manchester. I was very relieved when he approved it, for his own book on St Patrick is excellent. He followed the advice given by Daniel Binchy to writers on St Patrick: use the two authentic writings of the saint, the *Confession* and the *Epistle to Coroticus* as a valid basis for reconstruction.

Publishing with Michael Glazier

After the appearance of *Mediatress of all Graces*, Frank Duff suggested to me one day that I prepare another book on the subject. 'But,' he added, 'don't rush it, take your time.' I was perfecting my methodology and with this progress I was happy to be accepted in the two scientific reviews, *Marianum* and *Ephemerides Mariologicae* and one oriented to the apostolate, *Miles Immaculatae,* and in the proceedings of the International Mariological Congresses. I thought of the encyclopedia or dictionary format. I was not yet a reliable typist and I shudder slightly when I remember the disfigured copy which eventually went to the publisher.

I do not now recall how I succeeded in putting all the material together. I did a good deal of the work in Milltown Park Library, and used bits and pieces I had picked up here and there through the years. *Fabricando fit faber*. You learn by experience. A manuscript was ready after much toil and with the help of the published works of two of the outstanding Marian theologians of the present century: Gabriele Maria Roschini OSM, and René Laurentin.

My friend and colleague in the Pontifical Marian Academy, the American Carmelite Eamon Carroll, had mentioned to me a publisher named Michael Glazier. The name meant nothing to me at the time. Now I got the idea of writing to him to ask him if he would find my manuscript of interest. I sent it to him and eventually the details were ironed out. He launched it. He took particular care with the format and design, produced a handsome volume, entitled *Theotokos;* we had permission from the John Rylands Library, Manchester, to reproduce as a frontispiece the papyrus of the oldest prayer to Our Lady, the Greek which we render in Latin as *Sub tuum*.

The book, a large volume, appeared in 1982 and was reprinted in that year; it went into several editions, without counting the separate editions in the Philippines, to which we released it free of any royalty. It surprised us that the book sold; we were not too long out of the 'decade without Mary', the period of decline in Marian piety within the Catholic Church, when publishers were slow to risk their money on new titles related to Our Lady.

This was the beginning of my friendship with the man whom I regard as the greatest figure in Catholic publishing since Frank Sheed. Michael Glazier entered this world when a number of people thought it was crumbling – after the Council a number of American Catholic publishing houses closed down. The idea was that now 'Catholic' was old-fashioned, restrictive. Catholic authors should seek an outlet in the religious departments of the great secular publishing houses. Michael, Kerry-born, went against the tide, splendidly supported by his wife Joan. He had published a large collection of the early American Congress papers and he later brought out a selection of English state papers. But his real triumph was in Catholic collections and in the works of contemporary Catholic authors. He knew where to look for those qualified to advise on constructing series on Patrology or on the Bible. He also welcomed suggestions on older classics which had gone out of print.

Like all the truly great whom I have met, he makes it all look so easy, and he never seems in a hurry despite mounting demands on his time. I cannot imagine anyone being kinder or more sympathetic to an author, nor more courageous in facing unforeseen trials. On one occasion he was called to the telephone to learn that his entire three-story office building had collapsed into rubble. This would mean that manuscripts buried in the debris were lost. He wrote to me to tell me of my luck, which he and I attribute to Our Lady. He thought immediately, on receipt of the bad news, of the manuscripts of a second encyclopedia which I had sent him, *Trinitas*. With his friends he went along, knelt down and said a prayer. Someone noticed a page in the confused mass, and found the whole thing. For some reason before despatching the typescript in four packets I had inserted a little Miraculous Medal in each; I had never before done this with mail. Michael's advice was to continue and this I did. He took one such medal and pasted it into his address book. He went up to New York and came back to Wilmington, where he lived, minus the address book. But after some time it came back to him in the post, with a note which he sent me, saying 'Michael, Our Lady does not wish to be too long away from you. I found this on the sidewalk outside CitiBank.'

He had before long to face a terrible shock. The police telephoned to inform him that his secretary accountant had confessed to embezzling a large sum of money from him. I spare the reader the details of this story, for it also included thieving jewels in Wilmington shops. For Michael it led to the sale of his firm, published and future titles, to the Liturgical Press. He will not now engage in Catholic publishing; any books that he had brought out or commissioned will appear with an added imprint, A Michael Glazier Book. He was recently asked by the Liturgical Press to edit, with Monika Hellwig, a single volume Catholic encyclopedia. I was delighted to collaborate with thirteen articles.

Within a year of his retirement from publishing, Michael received three awards, something probably unique. The American Theological Society gave him a special award; the Catholic Biblical Association made him an honorary member – only four others have been so singled out; and the Catholic Library Association also presented him with a Gold Medal. All for exceptional services to the church.

Michael published two other encyclopedias for me, and had accepted a fifth, which came out with the imprint of the Liturgical Press, and the addition I have mentioned. I thank God and Our Lady for him; how many, if any, other publishers would have helped me so decisively?

4. Carmel

St Teresa of Avila

When Goethe came out of the Sistine Chapel he remarked that those who had not seen it could not have an idea of what a single human being could accomplish – not forgetting that it is but part of Michelangelo's achievement. Likewise I think that those who have not some acquaintance with the personality and written work of St Teresa of Avila cannot know how God can work in the depths of the human psyche, and how one individual could transcribe such an experience, disclosing depth upon depth of mystical reality. I have come to the opinion that outside the Bible, Teresa is the greatest woman who ever lived. Without any formal education she became one of the world's great writers. Devoid of human resources she established fifteen flourishing Carmelite monasteries, directed two other foundations. She did so in an age and in a country where female initiative was not only limited but practically excluded from the public domain, lay or ecclesiastic. She was the principal reformer of a whole order of men. She expounded a mystical theology which illumines this privileged sector of humano-divine knowledge astonishingly, and will continue to do so. She had a personal relationship with Jesus Christ possibly unequalled in the annals of women saints. And she was a totally fascinating human personality, the kind of person whom anyone deeply interested in the human species would like to meet.

Feminists complain that Teresa had to wait four centuries to be declared a Doctor of the Church; I understand their reaction. But there is another aspect to the event. Teresa is still, four centuries after she lived, one who captivates people. William Walshe's life, probably the best in English, the work of a great Hispanist, is read avidly. The great Anglican specialist in her work, as in that of St John of the Cross, Professor Allison Peers, by his very industry and skill as a translator, testified to her relevance to our times.

The Carmelite Order

I make no apology for this prelude to some memories I have to record of the Carmelite Order. In retrospect I see them all in the radiance of this amazing woman who rescued their convents from decline in her age, and assured them a permanent fountain of renewal, of spiritual vitality. Her daughters are at the heart of Catholic life as I could see in countries as different as Sweden and Kenya. They have faced the test of martyrdom, as in the French Revolution, the Spanish Civil War, or in Auschwitz.

St Thérèse of Lisieux

As a young priest I was influenced by the vast spiritual movement which originated in Lisieux in the early decades of the present century. A young girl, Thérèse Martin, had entered the Carmelite Convent where she died before her twenty-fifth birthday, having done nothing worthy of note – at least so some of her sisters in the convent thought. Thérése died on 30 September, 1897.

What I write is in the context of personal experience. Everyone has heard of the 'Shower of Roses'. Quite recently I came across an unusual example of this supernatural prodigality. Doing an article for the *Dictionnaire de Spiritualité* on the Anglican mystic, Evelyn Underhill, I read, in the course of her tribute to the saint, a rumour from the first world war to the effect that Thérèse had actually appeared in the allied headquarters and given the senior officers advice on their strategy. What I do know is that my uncle Walter wrote from the trenches that they were being helped by a Carmelite nun. It was a delight to see, in the Carmel of Lisieux, a side chapel dedicated to St

Michael to thank the saint for her assistance in their days of danger, a gift of Irish soldiers. It should be noted that St Thérèse was not beatified until 1923.

Thérèse Martin, at her entry to Carmel, had declared her purpose in choosing this vocation: to pray for the conversion of sinners and for priests. It was only after my ordination to the priesthood, on 25 July 1937, that I began to appreciate her personality and her spiritual doctrine. I was before long caught up in the movement within the church which drew its meaning and dynamism from her cult. Among the heartening things in this worldwide stirring of the supernatural was the commitment of the papacy. Pius XI is generally thought of in this context. He called her the 'star of his pontificate', said that she was 'a miracle of virtues and a prodigy of miracles,' beatified her in 1923, and canonised her in 1925. Like all her disciples I can tell at once that the first event took place on 23 April, the second on 17 May.

One should delay on Pius XI. For one thing he was the first Pope whose career we knew as it was unfolding. Communications were not closely adjusted to his predecessors in this century. Besides, he scarcely looked like one who would espouse the ideal of spiritual childhood, for he was elderly, tough, given it appeared to outbursts of temper, capable of withering retorts. 'The Cardinals are not happy with your single-handed negotiations of the Lateran Treaty, Holy Father; they think you should have consulted them.' 'Would you be a Cardinal if I had consulted them?' was the end of that dialogue.

Yet here was this old warrior, who had spent most of his life enclosed in libraries (the Ambrosian in Milan, and the Vatican) but who emerged to face the dictators unflinchingly, almost engaged in a spiritual love affair with the young French Carmelite, who was born when he was sixteen years of age and died twenty four years later. He dismissed the criticism that her doctrine was sentimental, if he ever heard of it. He saw the value of her essential intuition, an effect of the Gift of Understanding, that the Master disclosed a whole, creative, spirituality in the words, 'Unless you become as little children, you will not enter the kingdom of heaven' (Mt 18:3). The Christian life was not a pursuit of virtues leading to the perfection of love, but a process which must begin with love and grow to perfection from this beginning. The Pope had made the Catholic missions the great cause of his pontificate; he named St Thérèse Patroness of the Missions. He sent to Lisieux his secretary of State, Cardinal Pacelli who, he rightly thought, would succeed him, to give the inaugural blessing to the Basilica built with worldwide financial gifts, on the hill overlooking the town.

We were then conscious of backing at the highest level when we prayed to St Thérèse, or sought ever fuller understanding of her spiritual message. I joined the Association of Priests founded at Lisieux to help its members spiritually. I was fortunate, after completion of my theological studies, to visit Lisieux on the way home. I said Mass in the convent chapel and spoke to one of the nuns. That was just two months before the outbreak of war.

Two Irishmen and Lisieux

I was back in Lisieux in 1947. The town still bore the widespread damage inflicted by the heavy aerial bombardment; it was something of a wilderness. Intact within the ruins stood the Carmel. This was a miracle, for though requests had been made to the allied forces to spare Lisieux as much as possible, it was not within their power to bomb the town centre and leave one building untouched. They could and did spare the Basilica, which was well apart from the cluster of streets. A Catholic member of parliament instructed by Mgr John Power, an Irish priest in Birmingham diocese, a noted client of St Thérèse, had taken the necessary steps to ensure this happy outcome.

Another Irishman figured in the wartime events in Lisieux. For six weeks the sisters from the convent had been living in the crypt of the Basilica. I had heard a story current in Dublin that it was an Irishman, Lord Killanin, who had brought them back to their convent. I happened to find myself next to him at some meeting in Dublin and verified the story. Yes, he assured me, it was he. He was at the time a Brigade Major in the British army. He was with the detachment which reached Lisieux after the

German withdrawal. He asked his commanding officer to authorise use of army transport for this humanitarian purpose. Certainly, was the reply, and he was to have a 'whip-round' to raise money for a gift to the sisters. He was, he added, very happy to help the nuns since he had two aunts nuns.

Our neighbouring Carmelites

Living in Blackrock I had the happiness to know that there were two Carmelite convents in our neighbourhood, in Blackrock itself within fifteen minutes on foot, and in Kilmacud, not too far away, where I went sometimes on Sunday morning to celebrate Mass for the sisters and the few faithful who would come to the little side chapel open to the public. They later asked me to give a retreat in the convent, and also a Christian triduum. In the course of these visits I became acquainted with Mother Elias, a person of very great holiness. I was assured of her prayers, which in those early years in the priestly ministry I sorely needed. I visited her in her final illness when she was under the care of my close friend, Dr P. D. (Steve) O'Rourke. Her life was much influenced by the insight God had given her into his intimacy with the soul; it is expressed in a phrase she liked, *familiaritas stupenda nimis*. Now she has this intimacy unchangeably.

My contacts with Blackrock Carmel were for years not very frequent, in fact non-existent. As time passed it did come my way to celebrate Mass there if the chaplain required someone to take his place and made this request of the College authorities. I came to know one sister in particular, Sister Thérèse Gibbons.

Unlike her famous namesake, Sister Thérèse did not enter Carmel as a young girl. She had taught for some time in the upper-class Catholic convent school, Farnborough Hill, and was a friend of the great lady who dominated this institution for many years, Mother Roantree. Back in Dublin she became friendly with the city's most eligible bachelor, a doctor with magic radiance, handsome, idealistic, a spell-binder – Jim Magennis. When she informed him of her vocation his response was, 'I'll give you to God, not to anyone else.' She told me that one evening when they were at the theatre she suddenly saw on the stage a Carmelite convent cell. After her entry, he was given special permission to visit her, often engaging in lengthy conversations.

A vocation which began thus was sure to lead to the heights. Mother Thérèse did not falter. But she did not change her personality. She was very feminine, nobody's fool, very sensitive to ordinary people's problems, light-hearted, perhaps a little critical, not so much of the errant as of individuals whom she might find behaving a little bit above themselves. She liked to tease people and if by accident she came upon me reading something I had brought to give her, something of my own, she would cry out with some glee: 'Your favourite author, I suppose?'

That I received graces from God through the prayers and the very life of this saintly woman I have no doubt whatever.

Thérèse approached death with characteristic simplicity. She was not a stranger to pain, for she had had two operations for cataracts, the second a brilliant success, thanks to the skill of our mutual friend, Gearóid Crookes. In the last months memory wandered a little, so that visiting her was like talking to a little angel, detached, ethereal. The chaplain, Dr Desmond Connell, invited me to preach the homily at her funeral.

When Dr Connell was appointed Archbishop of Dublin ten years ago, he asked our superior to provide a chaplain for the Carmelites. I had the great joy of being appointed to the ministry. I do not doubt that Thérèse had a hand in the matter. It has been for me a pure joy to participate in the dedicated lives of these heroic individuals. This is not an easy way of life, certainly not in our time. What the world owes to the prayers offered in Carmelite convents we shall one day know to our astonishment.

Controversy

As an appendix to these brief memories I add a note on a controversial encounter I had on the subject of St Thérèse. A French priest living in England, Fr Etienne Robo, published a work on the saint in which, relying on alleged psychological principles, he seriously minimised her personal holiness. I challenged his findings in the pages of *Doctrine and Life*, a Dominican review of spirituality. He didn't like this at all. So there were further exchanges. What interested me was a report I had from a religious, a Paulist sister then working in the Lisieux bookshop, Sister Mary Bernard, of reactions inside the Carmel of Lisieux. One of the sisters remarked in the course of recreation that Fr O'Carroll had been too hard on Fr Robo. Sister Geneviève de la Sainte Face (Thérèse's sister Céline) disagreed. No one had the right to misrepresent her sister as Fr Robo had done. I was naturally gratified, not least because Céline's reply to a question during the canonical investigation prior to her sister's beatification gave me a thrill. 'Why do you want your sister beatified?' she was asked. In substance she answered, because people were afraid of God; they thought of him as a master or judge. Thérèse would convince them that he is a Father.

There had been allegations from time to time that the saint's autobiography was not genuine; that her sister, Mother Agnes, Prioress (for life by papal ordinance) had altered it! Eventually the Carmelites thought the only thing to do was to issue facsimile copies of all the saint's writings. People could see what had been changed. But one fact was incontrovertible: Thérèse before her death had fully authorised Agnes to make any changes she thought proper in the text. I, therefore, defended Mother Agnes in the pages of the Maynooth publication, *The Furrow*. The editor of the facsimile papers had written: 'the blank cheque was given'. The editor of *The Furrow*, Fr J. G. McGarry, wrote to me some time afterwards that Mgr Ronald Knox, translator of the Autobiography from the facsimile copy, in the course of a letter on some other matter, had stated that he agreed entirely with me. To answer the objection that the saint's portrait, the work of Céline, was not authentic, that it had been prettified, all the photographs preserved in Carmel were published. It would not surprise me to hear that someone objected to cloistered sisters being photographed so often! In some situations, with certain people, you cannot win.

The final word on St Thérèse is of celebration: 1997, her centenary year, saw her declared a Doctor of the Church.

5. Shrines

I

I must preface any account of shrines of Our Lady with a tribute to the French fathers who gave us in Blackrock College a chapel dedicated to Our Lady of Victories, the first in Ireland. The story of the Paris church at its origin is illuminating. The title goes back to Louis XIII, who built the church to thank Our Lady for favours he had received from her; he was the king who consecrated his realm to the Blessed Virgin Mary. In the early nineteenth century Catholic practice in the city area had declined almost totally. In the year 1838 the parish priest, Abbé Desgenettes, thought of going elsewhere. In this state of mind he heard one day a voice saying: 'Consecrate your parish to the holy and Immaculate Heart of Mary.' Despite initial doubt he was won over and did as he was told. His parish took on new life and from it was born the Archconfraternity of the Immaculate Heart of Mary, Refuge of Sinners, which was taken up in many countries.

The shrine has a special place in the history of our congregation. Francis Libermann cherished it, was convinced that through Our Lady of Victories he had received many graces. He said his first Mass there, assisted by Abbé Desgenettes. The parish priest was to introduce him to Bishop Barron who, accompanied by Libermann's missionaries, opened Africa to the faith – today there are one hundred million Catholics in the continent.

Blackrock College was brought into the radiance of Our Lady of Victories by the priest who founded it, Fr Jules Leman, a novice of Libermann's. The statue of Our Lady of Victories over the high altar in the college chapel has looked down on generations of students, many of whom were to be ardent apostles of Our Lady, Frank Duff, founder of the Legion of Mary, not the least of them.

It was after my ordination to the priesthood that I fully understood the importance of shrines, especially shrines of Our Lady. During my stay in Fribourg as a student in theology, I went from time to time to the local Marian shrine, Our Lady of Bourguillon, outside the town. It was a pleasant walk, crossing a high suspension bridge, then on through woodland. I do remember that once when Bishop Gerlier of Lourdes, later Cardinal Gerlier of Lyons, came to Fribourg and gave a public lecture, he mentioned the fact that he valued his daily visit to Our Lady of Bourguillon in place of the one he made to the grotto where St Bernadette saw Our Lady.

During holidays in Ireland after ordination, I went with an aunt, Sister Michael of the Marist Congregation, from Jamestown, Carrick-on-Shannon to Knock. I met Mrs Coyne who was working with her husband, Mr Justice W. D. Coyne, to secure recognition for this spot. We had, in a publication brought out by the Irish students in the university, drawn attention to the event in Knock.

I was to get to know Mrs Coyne very well in the years ahead. I became involved, some way or another, with the Knock Shrine Society in its Dublin membership, principally with a very committed Catholic and believer in the apparition, Countess Bernadette O'Byrne – her husband had the title of Papal Count.

Associated with the Countess was an English woman, Catherine Chatto, one of a great English Catholic family, widow of a famous Indian involved with Ghandi in the independence movement. She was, I think, the first person with a valid charism whom I met. She could tell you what was to happen to you in the future. She did so for others; she did so more than once for myself. Apart from such moments she was without the slightest trace of pious affectations; she was what we call down -

-to-earth, clear-minded, a lady. She could not, of her own volition, summon the gift. It came to her from time to time. She had been guided spiritually by one of the most exciting converts from the Anglican Church to Catholicism, Mgr Robert Hugh Benson.

Catherine's Irish friends were the O'Connors, the family of Rory, of whom I have written. Catherine believed that Rory kept a promise. She was at school with his sister Eily and used to spend holiday time with her; she and Rory were friends. They had made a pact that whichever of them died first would come back to the other.

On the occasion of a visit to Knock with these two friends, Catherine and Countess O'Byrne, I met the last surviving witness of the apparition living there, Pat Beirne. He was a gruff old gentleman. But if I had had any doubt about the authenticity of the event, he would have removed it by his testimony which was rock solid and utterly disinterested. No material advantage came to him from telling the truth and it was apparent that he sought none. He died soon afterwards. A Sister of Mercy in Castlebar Hospital, who knew that I had met him, wrote to tell me of his last wish. Whatever was left over from his savings, after funeral expenses, should go to Mass intentions. This came to one pound. He had his Masses.

II

Knock has changed enormously since those days, the war years. The successive archbishops of Tuam gave it increasing support. An event which occurred during the war showed that it was being seen as a national centre. Mass was celebrated on 18 August, 1940 for peace and the protection of Ireland; it had been preceded by a nationwide campaign of prayer. The Knock Shrine Society, due to the initiative of Mr Justice and Mrs Coyne, was growing in membership. The Society is composed of stewards and handmaidens, the former to assure orderly participation in the ceremonies, the latter caring for the sick who were coming to Knock in increasing numbers.

A turning-point in the life of the shrine was the appointment of Fr James Horan to Knock. He was one of the great priests of our time, a spiritual entrepreneur of genius. Fortunately the sixteen years he spent in Knock included the centenary year, 1979, and therefore the papal visit.

Everywhere one meets the evidence of James Horan's vision, courage, organising skill. The new Basilica, designed by Daíthí Hanly, is the principal element in the complex. There is also St Joseph's Hospice for invalid pilgrims wishing to stay; St John's for day care; there is a Blessed Sacrament chapel, a chapel of reconciliation, a museum.

Mgr Horan bought out those whose business premises were within the domain and those who held stalls along the main street. The entire domain is artistically landscaped, with Stations of the Cross well situated.

One of the great man's last projects was to attend to the cemetery, paying particular attention to the graves of the visionaries. The last time I saw him at Knock he took me to see it. Some time later I visited him in the Mater Hospital, Dublin, where, as I learned later, he came to think that his days were numbered. I heard the news of his death in France; he died in Lourdes. I spoke of him to my Sunday congregation in Chantilly. Judge their reaction when I told them that he had built an airport.

III

In the seventies I became acquainted with the shrine of Our Lady at Banneux in the Belgian Ardennes. A priest who had promised to accompany a group of pilgrims, mostly handicapped, was unable to go and asked me to replace him. I learned the story of Banneux later, but was initiated to the shrine apostolate at once. Irish pilgrims were coming there through the influence of two Catholic women of great character and piety, Mrs McCabe of Clones, mother of the playwright, Eugene, and Mme de Theux, of a Belgian noble family. Mme de Theux felt a strong attachment to Ireland through grateful memory of her governess, an Irish girl, Eileen Hanly. This splendid person showed her character during the first world war when Belgium was militarily occupied. She took the children who were in her care to London, borrowed money from relatives to help them survive, and brought them back safely to their country. She was an honoured member of the family and lived on, providentially as they thought, to care for the mother; they died within a week of each other.

Mme de Theux had travelled through Ireland to create interest in the shrine. Pilgrimages began, composed almost entirely of handicapped people and nurses. Their stay was planned as a retreat, a source of comfort and strength. There were lectures and regular religious exercises with the Mass as central.

Annual visits to Banneux deepened my understanding of the problem of pain in the Christian life. They enriched me with friendships notably that of Marie-Thérèse de Theux. Marie-Thérèse had the poise that often comes from noble ancestry, with a touch of light-hearted humour. Her dedication to the sick and handicapped, her attention to their every need in the wards of the Hospitalité, was one of the many instances I have seen that Christianity, when it is fully lived, is a source of true happiness.

Marie-Thérèse died at the age of fifty-seven. She had nursed her mother through a long illness, but still went on duty to Banneux for a triduum with invalids. She returned totally exhausted, was taken to hospital and, having received Holy Communion at a Mass celebrated in her hospital room, went peacefully to her reward. When I was called to the telephone by her aunt, who asked me to hear grave news, I wrongly thought: 'Marie-Thérèse's mother, despite all her devotion, has died.' It was a blow to friends of Banneux, for she had just become president of the Brussels branch and great things were expected. I felt it a duty to represent the Irish pilgrims at her funeral and to show solidarity with her family, who had given me much hospitality.

IV

I cannot write very much about Lourdes, which is for many the archetypal Marian shrine. I went there first in the early fifties with a very good friend, Vincent Kelly, a brilliant architect. He must have been inspired, for within a year he had to face the ordeal of cancer of the throat. He went through the post-operation pain – pain-killers are ruled out as the patient might swallow blood and suffocate – and the subsequent radium treatment, with courage. His faith was his support. The evening before he was to get the final result of tests, we played a few holes of golf in Dun Laoghaire. As I left him he said simply: 'If it's what we fear, you have no need to tell me it's for my good. I'll know that.' He remained faithful to this intuition.

I went back with Vincent and friends some years later. I had the good fortune to be in Lourdes for the International Mariological Congress and Marian Congress held in the city in 1958. The theme of the Mariological Congress was one destined to come into prominence before long in the deliberations, Our Lady and the Church.

The Marian Congress ended with a procession of all the participants through Lourdes. I noted that Mr de Valera was the only head of government taking part. The papal Legate was Cardinal Tisserant, who would be spoken of during the Council. His official address was on consecration to Our Lady. As a journalist I was given some time with him. He spoke very respectfully about Frank Duff.

I was in Lourdes thirty years later as a guest speaker at the world assembly held there that year by *Unum Omnes, The International Council of Catholic Men*, invited by the president that year, a past pupil of Blackrock College, the architect, Vincent Gallagher.

In many ways Lourdes speaks to me especially of Bernadette. There is something so attractive about her stark honesty. They wanted to make a little 'saint' out of her. When they told her to meditate she just said: 'I can't meditate.' But what was she doing when she spent long periods of silence sitting before a statue of Our Lady? Or when she, who had seen the reality and was dissatisfied with statues and images in the western style, could look on Icons with deep sympathy? Icons are instinct with the divine, revealing to faithful and theologians something of the mystery of the *Theotokos*.

Bernadette knew that she was chosen by Our Lady not because of who she was but because of who Our Lady was. Many other would say that, but there might be a tiny deep feeling: 'Well after all it was me'. I think that Bernadette was totally sincere. The decree on the heroicity of her virtue, an official Roman document, hinted that she was not always a paragon of perfection. Had the authors in mind her retort to the tiresome parish priest who pestered her with questions and finally asked: 'Was the Lady very beautiful?' 'Well, she was more beautiful than you'?

To offset that boutade I recall an incident worthy of a great saint. Before leaving Lourdes for the convent at Nevers, the little girl was one evening entering the local house of the same congregation. A man came out of the shadows to accost her. 'Bernadette, what was the Lady like?' he asked. Worn out with the same request, she was about to brush him aside. 'Bernadette,' he pleaded, 'I'm a sinner.' That won her. She gave him such an account of the one she had seen that he was converted.

V

I do not intend to write about all the shrines of Our Lady which I have had the good fortune to visit, but I would like to delay on Czestochowa, where I have prayed several times. There beats the heart of Catholic Poland. I would likewise find it easy to fill pages on other shrines taken as centres of piety in the countries wherein they stand – Walsingham in England, Mariazell in Austria, Einsiedeln in Switzerland, Loreto in Italy, the Basilica of the Immaculate Conception in Washington, Cap de la Madeleine in Canada.

Guadalupe is visited by twenty million pilgrims annually. Its distinctive origin and history should compel the attention of anyone interested in the history of humankind. I shall begin on a personal note. In December 1964 I was to travel to the United States. I was the companion of a baby boy adopted by American parents, one of the most beautiful children I have ever seen;

everyone who saw him expressed similar opinions. I was to visit the convents of the Poor Clare Sisters in California, invited to do so by their Abbess General, Mother Agnes of Newry. I would also meet my brother. Two nights before I left I decided to go on pilgrimage to Guadalupe.

One consoling factor was that I met a remarkable Irish priest, Fr Tom Fallon, who was living in Mexico. I hoped to make contact with him. By a freakish stroke of good luck, another name for Our Lady's intercession, I was able from the United States to send him a message announcing my arrival. What relief to see him cross the airport building and greet him. I felt safe. It was a few days before Christmas and Fr Tom, or 'Tommy' as he was affectionately known to his friends, brought me to the head house of his congregation and gave me hospitality there while I was in Mexico.

I have said that he was 'remarkable'. When I was with him he was in his early nineties, still active on the ministry. He was in Mexico because he had left his government post in Dublin over forty years previously to join a new religious society of priests, the *Missioneros del Espiritu Sancto*. It was founded at the height of the persecution in the early twenties by a Marist priest, instructed by a truly great mystic, Maria Concepción Cabrera de Armida 'Conchita'. Tom Fallon got to know of it through the British Ambassador in Mexico, Lord Greville, a member of an Anglo-Irish family. When he was in government service he had worked with Lord Greville, former Ambassador to Belgium, on the Belgian refugee problem during the first world war. The two remained in contact when the diplomat was appointed to Mexico.

Tom was a close friend of Frank Duff, and helped spread the Legion in the land of his adoption. Another friend of both was a Dublin business man, Matthew ('Matt') Lawlor, proprietor of a number of tobacco outlets in the city of Dublin. He became an associate member of the new society, was clothed in the habit when he died; he assigned a share of his profits annually to their funds, made the society his legatee.

Fr Tom's life had not lacked the spice of danger. He was ordained priest behind closed doors at three o'clock in the morning by a bishop exiled from his diocese. In his hospital ministry he worked with nurses who would alert him secretly when a patient was near death; he would enter as a visitor, in civil attire of course, and do his priestly work. His one fear if he was caught would be deportation; he carried a British passport and could not easily be imprisoned. Once he thought it was all over. He was caught and brought to court. But relief was instantaneous. The trial judge's wife was his spiritual disciple. He was let off with a 'severe' reprimand. How else could the judge face his wife?

So in his company I felt something of the heroic age. But like all heroes he was totally unselfaware. Diminutive in stature and wiry, he had sharp features, bright beady eyes; before smiling he would put on a mock serious face. A great friendship of his life was with 'Conchita'.

On the occasion of my first visit he brought me to see the miraculous image. He asked a priest seated nearby if I could go up on the altar close to it. 'As near as he likes,' was the reply, for this is the religious object most exposed to the public in the whole world. Early in the present century it survived a bomb blast – a stick of gelignite was hidden in a bouquet placed, at the donor's request, within eight feet of the framed Tilma. The crucifix was twisted, every window in the building was shattered, but the image remained intact, with not a scratch on the glass.

For the reader not acquainted with the story of the image, note that the material of the Tilma is woven grass. It should have perished in dust within forty years – that is four hundred and sixty-six years ago. It has taken on new life since Our Lady of Guadalupe was proclaimed Protectress of the Unborn. Why this title? Why is the image carried around the world by its guardian, Judge Daniel Lynch, halting ceremonially before abortion clinics? When this happened in Chicago, the directress came out, saw the image weeping, and decided to shut down the clinic. The woman depicted on the Tilma is young and pregnant. She wears the black belt which with the Aztecs was the sign of this state.

The Tilma is now in the newly built Basilica; the old one was in danger of collapsing from huge fissures in the walls. It was there that I saw it twice in recent years. On the first visit I had a delightful surprise. The lady who gave us hospitality, Senora Olga Azcarraga de Robles Leon, is a dedicated worker for the church. Almost by accident and seeking something to say, I asked her had she ever heard of an Irish priest named Tom Fallon. She could scarcely believe her ears. 'But you're talking about a very close friend of my family; he came to lunch with us every Sunday.' Later I was to learn from other members of the family that they all grew up in the protective shadow of his friendship. Olga knew all about his role in the *Missioneros,* his friendship with Conchita, his problems with one particular member of the society. His memory lasts vividly.

VI

I add a note on shrines of St Michael the Archangel. He likes high places. I have only viewed from the mainland nearby his lofty fastness off Kerry, Sceilg Mhíchil; thus too I honoured him in Mount St Michael off Cornwall. The miracle of nature and of art which accounts for Mont St Michel I have visited. How was it constructed? What problems in engineering! The stone was quarried inland, ferried in flat-bottom boats across the neck of sea, and hoisted eight hundred feet to the plateau. Then there was a masterpiece.

I relate a story certified to me by a French historian of architecture, Count Biver (known as biographer of Père Lamy). A Frenchman living in Paris, M. Martin, was one day visited by the Archangel, who complained that his sanctuary was in need of restoration. M. Martin must go to *La Croix*, the Catholic daily, and insert an advertisement seeking funds. The diffident gentlemen was warmly welcomed by the editor, who promised support. The funds came in, and the work of restoration was accomplished.

Then there was another apparition of St Michael. He would

like to have a suitable statue on the pin-point of the spire. M. Martin must go to a sculptor named Frémiet and ask for designs. The Archangel would choose the right one. Frémiet had been responsible for the statue of Joan of Arc on the Rue de Rivoli. The commission thrilled him and in due course from his designs the Archangel made his choice. I've seen a copy and the original through binoculars. It is superb, a fighter, with full weaponry and a coat of mail. Not so long ago it was done in gold leaf, as the surface may have been fading. Jacob Eppstein was equally delighted when he was asked to do the statue for St Michael's Cathedral, Coventry.

Monte Gargano has its legend and with thoughts of Padre Pio in mind – his monastery is not far away – I thanked God for giving us such a protector, as I did in Panormitti in the Greek Islands. There Monseigneur St Michel, as Joan of Arc called him, is a mighty presence, radiant with power.

VII

There are, as the reader may well think, large questions arising out of any mention or consideration of shrines, especially Marian shrines. We live in an age when apparitions of Our Lady are reported from many countries. I have mentioned that I met one of the witnesses to the Knock apparition. I also met Mariette Beco, the witness of Banneux. Others who figured in apparitions I was likewise fortunate to encounter; as yet there is no shrine to perpetuate their experience. Teresiana in the Philippines told me a story which, I hope, will not unduly shock the reader. She was a religious and said that she was favoured with apparitions of Our Lady. She was given a choice: she could retract this assertion or leave the convent. She refused to state what was false; so she left.

The Nuncio at the time organised opposition. When she went to see him he insulted her. Worse still, he put pressure on bishops to disavow her. Five signed a statement condemning her; four had never met her; one, on his deathbed, withdrew what he had stated, admitted that he had done so under pressure.

But there are cases of fraud. Certainly. In the twenties there was widespread interest in the alleged bleeding of a statue in the town of Templemore, in County Tipperary. The young man at the centre of the event was caught putting animal's blood on the statue. Not so long ago I saw a similar case exposed on French television. Again it was a statue, this time exuding oil. But the owner was seen steeping his hands in oil and laying this on the statue. The police moved in; he confessed everything.

How then shall we know what is genuine? How could I know when I met Patricia Talbot, the visionary of Cuenca, Ecuador? or Conchita Gonzalez the visionary of Garabandal? With Sister Agnes in Akita I had no problem; she is approved.

There are guidelines, some given by presentday church authority; one stated by the Lord himself. This is the test of the fruits: a good tree cannot bear bad fruit; a bad tree cannot bear good fruit. Typical fruits are conversion, miracles of healing, witness to the faith.

What may I seek in one claiming to have an apparition or a special divine communication? First that the claimant be completely normal, free of any mental defect. Only experts can pronounce with certainty on this question, to eliminate the possibility of flaws in the intellect, the imagination or the memory. Next is the question of truthfulness: is the witness utterly credible? Has he or she a record of complete reliability? Has he or she at any time deviated from the truth? Is he or she, consciously or unconsciously, prone or even partially liable to exaggerate or understate in reporting matters of personal interest.

There is then the question of transparency, which means that the visionary must convey the truth of God in an utterly disinterested way, with nothing of himself or herself interfering. From what I have written about St Bernadette, one can see how admirably she exemplifies this quality. She sought nothing whatsoever for herself in her testimony.

Next what is claimed to come from God or Our Lady must be in harmony with authentic church teaching, with the truths of the faith. Here too, St Bernadette shines. She did not understand the words Our Lady spoke to her. But they stated the doctrine of the Immaculate Conception solemnly defined four years previously by Pope Pius IX.

These criteria are directly related to the person or persons claiming a divine communication. May we not, in keeping with the teaching of Vatican II, look for the *sensus fidei*, the voice of the People of God? 'The whole body of the faithful who have an anointing that comes from the holy one (cf. 1 Jn 2:20-27) cannot err in matters of belief. This characteristic is shown in the supernatural appreciation of the faith (*sensus fidei*) the whole people, when, "from the bishops to the last of the faithful", they manifest a universal consent in matters of faith and morals.' (Constitution on the Church, 12)

Formerly critics might have asked, why does Our Lady appear in Europe, where the faith exists: why not in lands where the Gospel has not been preached, or where there are few believers? Now that she does appear in these regions and in so many other places, they ask: Why does she appear so often? Behind any such question there is a grave misconception. People think that Our Lady roams from one place to another; some may think that she is taking over the church.

Here it is necessary to emphasise that any apparition of Our Lady, being miraculous, involves directly an act of divine omnipotence. It is God, God the Holy Spirit, who effects the apparition. All is therefore to be attributed to divine wisdom. Our Lady does not act on her own. Her clients at different shrines throughout the world need not think that this in any way lessens her dignity, or her immense power with God. On the contrary, her unique role and dignity come from her utterly unrivalled intimacy with God.

Are the many Marian apparitions at the present time signs of a phase in history of the church which precedes the final decisive intervention of the Saviour? Only God can answer this question.

6. Ecumenism

I

Christian Unity is something we must work for and yet know to be beyond our power. In that it resembles the salvation of our souls. It depends on our efforts and without God's grace we cannot achieve it. Since there must be this indispensable element of divine grace at all times in the work for Christian unity, there is a continuous sense of mystery about it. It is with a consciousness of that mystery that I record my own feeble efforts in this mighty mission to which everyone bearing the name of Christ is called. No one looking to Jesus Christ as Lord can escape this imperative; it flows from the words of Jesus himself that there will be one Fold and even one Shepherd (Jn 10:16), from his prayer 'that they may all be one even as thou, Father, art in me and I in thee, that they also may be in us, so that the world may believe that thou has sent me.' (Jn 17:21)

I met the problem in my family, for I have Protestant relatives. I did not suffer from any prejudice, any sense of superiority in regard to those outside my communion. But I had no urge to do anything even to interest myself in Christian unity. In that I was like the overwhelming majority of students for the priesthood. The main thrust of theology, when the question of the church arose, was on the Catholic Church as the one true church. Though I did not know it then, the approach to the churches separated from Rome was a call to them to 'return' to the true church.

If there is implied criticism here, the criticism is easily over - simplified. The Catholic Church had many problems which seemed to claim priority: the missionary thrust to Africa was vital and absorbed interest and energy; open persecution showed itself in Mexico in the twenties and in Russia was active since the Revolution, though the Orthodox were the principal victims; the church in France took some time to recover from the official anti-clericalism of the first decade in the century; and the dictators came to stride Europe in the twenties and thirties, their onward march echoing dangerously through the Catholic world.

Then came the war. Christians were in places seen to make common cause, not only in the prison and concentration camps. The war ended and things seemed to revert to their pre-war situation. Pius XII had taken an initiative in launching an association called *Unitas* in Rome; there was a review with that name to spread the idea. Not much followed by way of direct result. Thus things stood until John XXIII and Vatican II.

During the war years I was much involved in a highly fruitful ecumenical initiative in Dublin. Why this was so and how it fared I shall tell in more detail in the chapter of this book which deals with Dr McQuaid. I take up the story before and after Vatican II. As I have already said, I was at the time much involved, as regards writing and also publishing, with the *Catholic Standard* and *The Leader*. I gave free rein to my admiration for John XXIII. I also dealt with his momentous decision to summon a General Council in a short work I wrote about him at the outset of his pontificate.

The announcement was made within three months of his election, on 25 January, 1959; it took most people unawares. He spoke then of church unity. This ideal, this hope he spelled out in his first Christmas address: 'And the vexing problem of the broken unity of the heritage of Christ still remains, and obstacles still hinder its solution. It will be a long road of burdening difficulties and uncertainties. The sadness of this sorrowful observation does not arrest, nor will it arrest, we hope to God, the effort of our soul to continue the loving invitation to our dear separated brothers, who also carry on their forehead the name of Christ, who read his holy and blessed gospel, and who are not insensible to the inspirations of religious piety.'

John XXIII recalled the invitations to unity of his predecessors from Leo XIII to Pius XII, then went on: 'permit us – by which we mean to say, will you permit us? – to say that we intend to pursue humbly but fervently our duty urged upon us by the words and example of Jesus, the divine Good Shepherd, which he continues to speak to us in the vision of the harvests which whiten the vast missionary fields.' The Pope then recalled the words of the Master from the allegory of the Good Shepherd (Jn 10:16) and the priestly prayer (Jn 17:21). There is more than a nuance of difference in the declaration of intention and the 'invitation', which had been the papal approach previously.

II

I am not narrating church history and have no need to follow the steps taken by the Pope and his collaborators to further his plan. I was in Rome early in 1961 to prepare some programmes for Radio Eireann on the preliminaries of the Council. The preparatory Consilia were already quickly named and among them was a Secretariat for Christian Unity, a complete innovation – it remains, as is well known, to this day. I spoke to its head, Cardinal Bea, who was then at the beginning of his high-profile career as an ecumenist. He was a biblical scholar, had helped draft one of the great documents which opened the way for the teaching of Vatican II, Pius XII's encyclical on the Bible, *Divino Afflante Spiritu* (1943). Bea later pointed to two other encyclicals from Pius which had a similar effect, *Mystici Corporis Christi* on the church (1943) and *Mediator Dei* on the liturgy (1947).

The Cardinal was in happy mood when I talked with him. One point he made with firmness. The language of 'return' of the separated brethren was not henceforth a desirable mode of expression.

I had meetings also with Cardinal Tardini and Cardinal Agagianian, the former Secretary of State, the latter Cardinal Prefect of the Congregation for the Propagation of the Faith (now for the Evangelisation of Peoples). I spoke a good deal to Cardinal Tardini about Pius XII. When I mentioned the separated brethren the great man – for thus, with some knowledge of his career, I consider him – advised me to go cautiously. That would have been the normal reaction within the Curia, very understandable. If anyone feels like criticism, let him examine his own conscience on what he has done.

Cardinal Agagianian was an Armenian of the Catholic rite. He was a person of exquisite manners, a sheer delight to meet. He told me that Christian unity *vis-à-vis* the Orthodox would not be easy; he did put it more strongly than that. I mentioned before leaving him that we were having a Patrician Congress in Dublin in summer of that year. Would he not be a likely Papal Legate? He begged me not to mention it elsewhere, which I promised. I think he wanted to come and feared that an advance account of it would ruin his chances. He was appointed and I met him very briefly, to offer him a copy of my book on Fr Leen, whom he had publicly praised. He was later named one of the Moderators of the Council sessions. He was acting in this capacity when a vote was taken in the assembly in October 1963 on whether Our Lady would be treated in a separate constitution or in a chapter as part of the Constitution on the Church.

We rejoiced at the passing of the Decree on Ecumenism in the Council, and at the many references to ecumenical activity in other documents. What then could we do when the Council sessions ended in 1965? I have little to report in answer to this question. As a member of the Pontifical Marian Academy I attended the International Mariological Congresses which it has organised; I have been present and read papers at some of them since 1975. That held in Saragossa in 1979 initiated dialogue between Catholics and the members of other churches present as guests. This practice continued at the subsequent congresses held in Malta and Kevalaer. In these statements the subject was doctrinal and devotional attitudes to Our Lady. The meetings were characterised by friendliness and mutual understanding. In doctrine there was much common ground. The parting of the ways was generally at the point where invocation of Mary was raised. Catholics and Orthodox think this normal. Protestants find it unacceptable. If there seemed to be stalemate in dialogue, there was clarity in exposition of the confessional beliefs.

III

We had known in Ireland of a venture that seemed by definition doomed to failure, the Ecumenical Society of the Blessed Virgin Mary. It was a success. The principal agent in this strange turn of events was a layman, a convert to Catholicism, Martin Gillett. He proceeded from the simple truth that the Mother of Christians would want to see her children united. When I say 'seemed by definition doomed to failure' I recall the general Protestant distrust of Mary, which would seem to resist or simply ignore a body bearing her name as a title. This did not happen. With the expansion of the Society in Britain and the United States, there was evidence that Protestants were willing to engage in dialogue about Our Lady and to participate in common prayer in which she would be honoured.

After some contact with the Society in England, an Englishman lecturing on Irish in University College, Dublin, Nicholas Williams, stirred interest in extension to Ireland. When it was clear that there would be sufficient members to form a branch in Dublin, an inaugural date was fixed. Dom Alberic Stacpoole, OSB, a monk of Ampleforth and president of the Society, came over for the meeting. The Rev John Neill (later Church of Ireland Bishop of Tuam), at the time in charge of St Bartholomew's church, Clyde Road, allowed us to use his parish hall.

That was in 1981. We have continued, with meetings spaced over the year and an annual general meeting. We have invited lecturers competent to speak on themes relevant to Christian unity. We have not so far succeeded in attracting large numbers, nor in gaining many members among the clergy. We do our best in hope. Our greatest moment was the International Conference which we hosted at Easter 1984 in Blackrock College, where meetings are generally held. Lecturers at the general meetings of the Conference represented a wide spectrum. Bishop Kallisthos

Ware was present, as were others of the Orthodox world. Ross McKenzie was impeded at the last moment by illness demanding surgery. An American Presbyterian, he was to have spoken on Our Lady of Guadalupe! His fellow Presbyterian, Donald Dawe, spoke on the Immaculate Conception.

A challenging contribution was made by Bishop Richard C. P. Hanson, the patristic scholar, one-time Church of Ireland Bishop of Clogher, at the time assistant Bishop of Manchester and Professor in the School of Divinity in Manchester University. He spoke on Mary in the Bible and he surprised me by his fundamentalist opinions. He was received with the greatest courtesy, and I made it clear that what we wanted to hear was Bishop Hanson's views, not Bishop Hanson saying something to please us. He was delighted and in thanking us added: 'I thought you might lynch me.' Leaving the hall he turned to me and remarked: 'You have given me something to think about.' In a letter of thanks he said the same thing. He was, during his stay with us, very popular with everyone. Honesty was his hallmark, as I recall from the old days of the Mercier Society. I must add a touching detail which shows his ecumenical concern. He had done much research and reflection on Origen and published work on him. This brought him into close relationship, through scholarly meetings, with the great French expert on Origen, Henri Crouzel, SJ. Dr Hanson's magnum opus, on which he had been working for a long time, appeared just at the time of his mortal illness; it was entitled *The Search for the Christian God*, a study of Arianism and related questions. It was dedicated to Henri Crouzel!

IV

Early in 1982 I was asked by the secretary of the Irish hierarchy to arrange, with the Rev Robert G. England of the Church of Ireland, an inter-church Study Group which would report to the Ballymascanlon Inter-Church Conference on Marian devotion. The stated purpose was that we may 'deepen our knowledge of one another and ...understand each other's faith and practice more accurately'. We had no difficulty in assembling a joint group composed of two members of the Church of Ireland, Rev Robert G. England and Canon Edgar Turner, two members of the Presbyterian Church, Rev John Thompson and Rev Alan Flavelle, one representative of the Methodist Church, Rev Johnston McMaster, five Roman Catholics, Rev Brian Nolan, CM, Rev Christopher O'Donnell, O Carm, Sister Céline Mangan, OP, Dr Donal Flanagan and myself.

We met five times between April and December 1982. The first meeting was in Blackrock College; thereafter Mount Oliver, the Catechetical Centre near Dundalk, was more convenient as some members lived in Northern Ireland. Our report was completed by 14 January, 1983. The meetings were marked by total mutual trust and comprehension. There was an abundance of knowledge and experience in the whole group.

I can but give an outline of the report. We summarised briefly the beliefs held in common by all the churches and then set forth a statement on each of the churches from those representing them within our group: Mary in the Presbyterian Church; Mary in the Methodist Church; Mary in the Church of Ireland; Mary in the Roman Catholic Church. We identified the problem areas and we suggested practical measures. Having re-read the report while writing this, I think that it would be very desirable to have it in print and available to the public.

V

Perhaps I may mention here an encounter I had with one of the great ecumenists of the century, Patriarch Athenagoras. He was the first Ecumenical Patriarch to meet a Pope for centuries. The Ecumenical Patriarch resides in the Phanar, in Istanbul. His primacy is not one of jurisdiction, but of honour. Much depends on the personality of the man, for the number of Orthodox Christians in Turkey is tiny; there are still less Catholics.

To meet such a mighty figure would be an event in one's life. I was introduced to him by some members of the Legion of

Mary in Istanbul. I was to be at his residence on 24 June (the year was 1969) in mid-morning. He sent for a treat to offer me, something like ice-cream. We chatted, if the word is not disrespectful. He had in his hand a telegram which he read for me. It was from Paul VI thanking him for his message of congratulation; it was the Pope's feastday, as he was baptised John the Baptist Montini. Then to my surprise and delight he invited me to lunch with him. Would I mind waiting with some friends while he completed the morning's business?

The Patriarch spoke to me about his hopes for the future. He looked forward to the moment of communion between Orthodox and Catholics. He had made history by flying to Jerusalem in 1964 to meet Paul VI, and, in the following year, joining solemnly with the Pope to rescind mutually the excommunications which had, in 1054, caused the schism. Henceforth, as the Pope made clear in giving the example, we can speak of 'Sister-Churches'; John Paul II can speak of the hope he has of the church 'breathing with its two lungs.' Patriarch Bartholomew said to me, in an interview, to which I shall refer later, that Athenagoras I did for the Orthodox what John XXIII did for Catholics: he opened the way for mutual understanding between the churches.

At table, during lunch, the Patriarch was relaxed, teasing, affectionate. He asked me would I like to be his secretary. Would I? 'Who are the policemen in New York city?' he asked me – he had spent eighteen years there, speaking English fluently. I suggested that they were Irish. He concurred and immediately spoke of their integrity, 'very upright men!'

As we parted the great man regretted that there was no photographer; so did I. I shall never forget the impression he made on me of sheer majesty, yet majesty clothed in Christian simplicity.

7. France

I

I have spent most of my life in Blackrock College, which is a French foundation, a community in a religious congregation closely linked with France. The head house was in Paris, not Rome, until the sixties of the present century. The first founder of this congregation was a Breton nobleman, Claude Poullart des Places (d. 1709), a close friend of St Louis-Marie Grignion de Montfort. His religious institute was, in 1848, united with a new missionary society, under the patronage of the Heart of Mary, founded by a convert Jew, the spiritual writer Francis Libermann, the one to whom God gave the intuition of Africa's Christian future and the courage to pioneer its realisation.

It is of interest to us to know that the Frenchman who led the group of fathers who began the congregation in Ireland was a novice of Libermann, Fr Jules Leman. He came, as did members of other French religious congregations, to lead Irish boys and girls from the cultural vacuum in which they lived despite Catholic emancipation. Thanks to the sure research and published work of a great historian, Fr Sean Farragher, my colleague in the College, we may not forget our debt to these French founding fathers. Fr Leman's success was so great that his death was described as a national tragedy by a high government authority.

Indirectly or directly, members of the Irish province have come under French influence to their advantage; directly with Bishop O'Gorman, whom I have mentioned; still more so perhaps with the apostle of Nigeria, Bishop Joseph Shanahan, who founded or inspired three missionary institutes; he received his entire education in France. When I think of him in this context I call to mind the greatest American bishop of the nineteenth century, John Ireland of St Paul, similarly favoured.

I could imbibe French culture in Fribourg. I was later given the opportunity to come closer to the French church when I was called to replace in summer time an Irish priest working in France. Tom Freyne was one of those who volunteered, in the thirties, to work in French dioceses. He was in the senior seminary for Beauvais when war broke out; he had to return home. His studies were completed in St John's Seminary, Waterford. Thereupon he went straight to London and offered his services as a chaplain to the Free French Forces. They could not accept him as he was not a French citizen, so he went to the RAF where he had a distinguished career, retiring with the rank of Honorary Wing Commander. He then went to his French diocese.

II

Fr Tom was *curé* of a country parish, Guiscard, near Noyon, when I first replaced him. I got to know many people, several families in the area, for to Guiscard were joined two other districts which had once been parishes, Maucourt and Quémy. I found these people very hospitable, cooperative, above all devoted to their *curé*. I naturally thought of the *Diary of a Country Parish Priest* by George Bernanos, without the slightest desire to emulate him. Guiscard was a very pleasant change from life in an Irish secondary school. The village church, centuries old, was an architectural gem, as were the outlying churches, one of which was 'classified'. So were wood carvings in Guiscard church; I felt, as I think did Fr Tom, that the whole building should have been so honoured. I cannot mention names, though some I would want to, for as I got to know the parish and its wonderful people, my response was one of admiration. This was not the France of hasty ill-informed generalisations; this was reality, the stuff of life, unaffected, unspoiled. The department was l'Oise, but the region was Picardie, evocative for anyone like me whose relatives had fought in the first world war.

One of my priest friends, *curé* in a neighbouring parish, was a Breton, François le Pévedic. The priests in the immediate vicinity met every Tuesday in his presbytery for a meal and he would get one of them to fetch me; all of them treated me as one of themselves. It was priestly solidarity, mutual support, salutary.

Some years ago Fr Tom withdrew from Guiscard to another assignment. He is chaplain to the Fondation Condé in Chantilly. The Fondation Condé is a complex comprising a hospital for elderly invalids and a separate establishment where people are received as guests. The Condé implies a royalist connection and in fact the patron and director is the heir to the French throne, the Comte de Paris.

Chantilly is well known in the racing world, though the emphasis is on training, with of course some prestigious meetings in the very fine race course. It is beautifully situated and the chateau is high on the tourist circuit. Its attraction for me was Les Fontaines, a former Rothschild property, then a Jesuit seminary, now a cultural centre directed by the Society. It has one of the finest theological libraries in Europe, and this was a fifteen minute walk from the chaplain's apartment, a walk through a pleasant park.

I was at the time engaged on much beavering for the encyclopedias which Michael Glazier, and then the Liturgical Press, were publishing. The resources of this great centre were invaluable to me. I received here, as I received in two other great Jesuit libraries, Milltown Park in Dublin and the Bollandistes' library in Brussels, courtesy and generous assistance which I cannot over-praise. The Society of Jesus is deservedly famous for its libraries. In each of the three best known to me the librarian was a friend: Fr Dermot Fleury in Milltown, Fr Cerckel in Brussels and Fr Robert Brunet in Chantilly.

With Fr Brunet I had an amusing relationship. He called me *l'homme au parapluie* – he even once suggested to the secretary that she classify my reader's ticket under the letter P! If I wrote to him requesting a photocopy of some material – which, of course, I got at once – he would sign R. Brunet and draw a little umbrella beside his name. His dedication to his work, his generosity with his time, his ability to track down a bibliographical item, were uncanny. When I reached Les Fontaines the year that he had left through illness, I felt that I was walking in a void.

III

Since, as I have stated, I was doing some work for the *Dictionnaire de Spiritualité,* I felt still more at home in Les Fontaines. Fr Rayez resided there, as does Fr André Derville. What work these men accomplished! Seeking authors for the different articles, handling the manuscripts, arranging for proof-reading, and finally seeing it all through the printers: it all demands endless, careful labour. I always got proofs in two stages. The end result was always word perfect.

Since I am talking about French culture, I add two points which occur to me in the context of Les Fontaines. It is as I have said, a cultural centre, affording facilities to a variety of Catholic and other religious groups for seminars, encounters of different kinds, sometimes at a very high level. Secondly the *Dictionnaire* to which I was honoured to contribute is in a great French tradition, to which I and so many other are indebted. The French have excelled in encyclopedias of this kind. The *Dictionnaire de théologie catholique* is a vast treasure-house of knowledge; it is equipped now with lists giving references and cross-references to the entire set, indispensable to research workers.

An ongoing multi-volume work, *Catholicisme,* provides information not only on Catholics important enough to arouse intellectual curiosity, but on persons and themes interesting to Catholics. A very valuable *Supplément* in several volumes has appeared to the *Dictionnarie de la Bible.* I should add the *Dictionnaire d'Histoire et de Géographie Ecclésiastiques* and the *Dictionnaire des Philosophes.* There are already available in well known collections the writings of the Greek and Latin Fathers of the church. *Sources Chrétiennes* (1940ff.) rendered a service in providing individual works of the Fathers in books of medium, easily accessible format, each carrying a French translation of the original text, the editing in the hands of a specialist. The collection continues and helps those who realise that the Fathers of the church are henceforth vitally important to the faithful who can read them.

8. Archbishop John Charles McQuaid

I

Dr McQuaid died in 1973 after a long episcopate, and a period of retirement, in a well-known diocese. I lived in Dublin during his rule of this diocese. I had an opportunity to know him in the previous phases of his life; I came under his influence in Blackrock College from 1925 when he joined the staff, until 1928 when I left to go to the Novitiate of the Congregation to which I belong. I had occasional brief contacts with him in the intervening years before my return to Blackrock College in 1939. He had just ceased, in that year, to be superior of the community and president of the college, and had taken up his duty as dean of the final year, residing in a separate house known as the Castle.

I begin with my first distinctive memory of this man. But I must set the framework. Some time after the academic year 1925-26 had begun, important changes in the staff were announced. An elderly priest, Fr Michael Downey, had been replaced as president by Fr Edward Leen, about whom I have written, and Fr Leen's place as Dean of Studies would be taken by a priest summoned from Rome, Fr McQuaid.

In fact, I learned afterwards, Fr McQuaid had interrupted the course for which he had been sent to Rome, Sacred Scripture at the Biblical Institute. Though his studies were cut short he was able to obtain a doctorate in theology from an examining board still functioning with power to grant this degree. His late arrival was due to a hasty adjustment to a new programme of studies.

I remember vividly after seventy years a special moment for me after this gifted man's arrival in the college. I was standing near the study hall at the foot of the stairs which led to our Director, Fr Bertie Farrell's office. The new priest passed by. He seemed to have some aura or atmosphere about him that was unusual. It was just his appearance. His features were finely chiselled, his bearing was reserved but full of dignity. Serenity and the sense of one living mostly within. A hint of mystery, which scarcely declined through the vicissitudes of later years.

It was for me the beginning of hero-worship. I had the good fortune to have Fr McQuaid as Professor of English Literature for three years. He took full advantage of the freedom from prescribed texts given by the new curriculum to introduce interesting items into our daily classes.

This was a born pedagogue, inspiration and instruction blended in one. Our English literature class became a liberal education. In fifth year, then a relatively free interval between the Intermediate and Leaving Certificates, the course spread out to include some elementary aesthetics, some philosophy, and up-to-date information on contemporary Catholic literature. Those were the days when Hilaire Belloc and G. K. Chesterton were Catholic literary idols. We heard a good deal of both, all rendered magnetic by the elegant diction of the reader. I remember that as G. K.'s poem *Lepanto* appeared, we heard it in the classroom: 'White founts falling in the courts of the sun' and the words which the teacher seemed to cherish, 'dim drums throbbing in the hills half heard.' Chesterton's use of alliteration and assonance just delighted him.

Other readings figured on the menu, from Newman, or from a recently published book by William O'Brien, *Irish Fireside Hours*, or *The Masterful Monk* by Owen Francis Dudley. Nor must I forget Fr McQuaid's blackboard script. I have never seen classroom lettering so impressive.

II

I came back to the college as a priest member of the community in 1939. There were newcomers in the college administration. Fr

John English, a Tipperary man who had spent all his priestly life in Trinidad, acquiring there a very great reputation as an educationalist, was now brought back as superior to Blackrock; Fr Con Daly, a past pupil and past prefect of the college, had come from Rockwell where he had been Dean of Studies, to take up this post in his *Alma Mater*.

The author of these changes, which caused some surprise, though within Constitutions of the Congregation, was the Provincial, Fr Daniel Murphy ('Dr Dan'). He was, as I have written, a Kerryman, a strong personality. He also had an impressive record as Dean of Studies in Rockwell, which had been recently threatened with closure, but which he brought to the head of examination results in the country during his tenure of office.

Fr McQuaid did not find it easy to leave the office of president. During his nine years at the head of the community and college staff he had acquired a certain prestige beyond its walls. He had hosted the Garden Party for the International Eucharistic Congress in 1932. He was elected chairman of the Catholic Headmasters' Association, which made him a key figure on an influential circuit. He had contacts with the Archbishop of Dublin and with the Apostolic Nuncio, Archbishop Paschal Robinson, OFM.

III

Dr McQuaid had developed a very close relationship with Mr De Valera, whose residence was on Cross Avenue, in the rear of the college property. Mr De Valera was a past pupil, who had had as classmates Cardinal D'Alton and James A. Sweeney, a member of the judiciary in India, and among his contemporaries, Alfred O'Rahilly. He had a lifelong attachment to the college, where his sons were educated also. The eldest of these, Vivian, had a tendency to asthma and Dr McQuaid had been good to him; he allowed him stay on in a room in the college, in a wing apart from the main building, during his university studies, because in the college he was free of asthma. Before the boy's father had been elected to office, Vivian, somewhat isolated among boys mostly sympathetic to the opposite political party, had been protected by Dr McQuaid.

Mr De Valera took advice from his priest friend on certain practices of piety. Years after his successful agreement with Chamberlain on the return to the Irish State of the ports still held by the British, he went to Lisieux and told the sisters, one of whom was Mother Agnes, sister of St Thérèse, that he had carried a relic of the saint on his person during the negotiations. Whether he received the relic from Fr McQuaid or not, the action would have been in harmony with an orientation he seemed to accept from him. Thus the priest introduced him to one of his own favourites in the heavenly court, a French priest who in life had enjoyed visions of Our Lady, Père Lamy. Dev went on pilgrimage to the scene of Père Lamy's labours. A church built in the Latin quarter in Paris as a result of certain charismatic events in the life of a young French girl, Olive, Sister Mary of Christ the King, had as one of its bells Marie-Irlande. It was the gift of Mr De Valera, informed by Fr McQuaid.

The most significant effect of Dev's friendship with Fr McQuaid had been in the drafting of the Constitution which was submitted to the Irish people in 1937. Years later, at a meeting in Aras an Uachtaráin, the presidential residence, where his guests were members of the Holy Ghost Congregation, Dev said that he wished it to be known that the sections of the Constitution which had been most admired, those dealing with the family and social order, owed much to the Holy Ghost Fathers. That meant Fr McQuaid. To what extent that meant Fr Denis Fahey, a mentor of his, is a matter for recondite research. Fr Fahey publicly criticised the Constitution for not proclaiming the Catholic religion the religion of the state, as the Spanish Constitution of 1953 would do later.

IV

I return to Fr McQuaid, reduced from a position where he was holding levers effective on a national scale to a subordinate post in secondary school life. He had grown used to power in a wider context. He had at least one former associate working discreetly to reverse the demotion. Fr English, as a result of this activity, flew to Paris to resign the office so that Fr McQuaid could be reinstated. The Superior General, a resolute Breton, Mgr Louis le Himsec, would have none of it. He was being appealed to over the head of the Provincial, which did nothing to promote harmony at a high level in the Province. There always had been some unspoken rivalry between Dr Murphy and Dr McQuaid. It would come up again.

How did I find my former hero, now that I was theoretically his equal? The presence was still striking; he stood out in any group. The interest in things aesthetic persisted. As president he had adorned the college chapel and other buildings with notable artistic works, stained glass by Michael Healy and Hubert McGoldrick, and minor works by Evie Hone, whom he had received into the Catholic Church. Her principal contribution to our stained glass would come later – a three-light window on the theme of Pentecost fittingly donated to the Castle Oratory by the past students to mark his appointment as Archbishop. While Dean of the Castle Dr McQuaid prompted the order of a beautiful set of Stations of the Cross in carved Italian lemon wood. And he secured an interesting item of marble sculpture, a piece depicting a dead knight.

Conduct of things academic in the Castle was orderly, efficient. Dr McQuaid's influence on the boys living in the same house as him was notable. The idea of a separate house for the final year had been his innovation. It was to afford a 'generous measure of controlled freedom', to borrow his own phrase. Now, in its second year, he was the one to put this slightly ambiguous ideal into practice: to ease the transition from the rigid discipline of secondary school to the freedom the boys would have as third-level students. Different schools had over the years noted failures in the adjustment.

Curiously, though living in the same house and occupied

with one class which was under his control, I had little to do with Dr McQuaid in the year and three months which intervened before his appointment as Archbishop of Dublin. I thought he had changed from the young priest whom I had so admired. I thought he was very conscious of his achievement. But, despite one unfortunate incident, when he treated me disrespectfully before the boys in my class, he was considerate and helpful.

The appointment as Archbishop caused joy to his admirers in the Province, for a moment something short of consternation in the diocese. Who was responsible? A key figure in the preliminaries may have been Joseph ('Joe') Walshe, Secretary of the Department for External Affairs, later Ireland's first Ambassador to the Holy See. Joe was approached by someone who had influence with him, who told me of his démarche. He reacted favourably. Letters were sent to the Nuncio and Dev himself was exposed to some pressure. He may very well have been waiting for this, since he thought so highly of Dr McQuaid. He is said to have made his preference known at the Vatican. Obviously his voice would carry weight. All things being equal, it is to the Holy See's advantage to have as bishop in the capital city of a Catholic country, the seat of government, a prelate totally acceptable to those in power.

V

Dr McQuaid was the first member of his congregation appointed to a European diocese – a Portuguese Holy Ghost Father was similarly honoured later. He was the first religious since Archbishop Troy, OP (d. 1823). The Archbishop of Armagh, Cardinal McRory, came to Dublin to act as principal concelebrating bishop. This had not happened for centuries, that Armagh would so honour Dublin. Gelasius of Armagh had consecrated St Laurence O'Toole in 1162.

The auspices could not be better. The diocesan clergy rallying quickly showed no sign of resentment or opposition. In the light of subsequent history, one of the many expressions of congratulation has a certain irony. The governing body of the Royal College of Physicians, to mark one hundred years' connection between Dr McQuaid's family and the medical profession, presented to him an item from the college museum, a Borgia ring; the president that year was a distinguished Protestant physician, Dr Rowlette.

I am not giving, even in summary form, a history of Dr McQuaid's tenure of the episcopal office. I write mostly in a frame of personal reminiscence. I was present at the consecration in the Pro-Cathedral on 27 December, 1940. I lost sight of the one elevated above us for some time. I did receive an autographed photograph for the College Scout Troop, to which I was chaplain at the time.

I incurred his displeasure for a long while. The reason was my interest in Protestants and Jews. I must elaborate on that statement of cause and effect. During my years in Fribourg I had come under the influence of one of the great bishops of the time, Mgr Marius Besson. To give an idea of his stature I quote a remark by the prestigious Canon (later Cardinal) Cardijn: 'I wish to thank Mgr Besson for having covered the J.O.C. with his prestige throughout Europe.' This prelate was the outstanding episcopal ecumenist in the Catholic Church between Cardinal Mercier and Vatican II, possibly because he was the only one.

Bishop Besson was a historian. His ecumenical ideas were expressed in two books which we read avidly: *La route aplanie* and *Après quatre cents ans*. He was the first bishop to order his priests to use *Nos frères séparés*, forbidding the word Protestants. This was a courageous innovation since his diocese comprised the Protestant cantons of Vaud and Geneva. But personality makes its presence felt. The bishop was a magnificent orator and the students in Fribourg loved him. We would find him sitting beside us in the library (it was cantonal and university) beavering away quite simply. We would meet him in the streets, a pedestrian like ourselves.

With my head full of such a memory I found it easy to participate in the Sunday retreats for non-Catholics organised by the

Legion of Mary. They were often held in Blackrock College, welcomed there originally by Dr McQuaid when he was president. These retreats, which attracted the most interesting people, were geared to those who might wish or be prepared to consider becoming Catholic.

VI

Out of this movement something different grew. This was the Mercier Society. The motto was *Towards Mutual Understanding*. Those of what we now call the separated churches were invited to meet Catholics with a view towards a free exchange of views on subjects of common interest, on which there might be divided opinions. A suitable structure was quickly developed. There were two committees, Catholic and Protestant, and a joint group where representatives of both sides met to plan the meetings.

The format of the meeting was simple. A paper was read by the speaker for the night, speakers alternating from each side. After a tea-break, there was open discussion. Utter frankness was the rule and this was maintained with great goodwill. Only two unpleasant incidents occurred during the session and in each case the one responsible was a speaker from England: Fr Hugh Pope, OP, referred to some Anglicans of the early days as a 'dastardly crew', while the Rev W. ('Billy') Matthews, Dean of St Paul's, made a disparaging remark about Pius XII. Apologies were mutually made and accepted.

The success of the Society was far more striking than any of us foresaw. There were two future bishops of the Church of Ireland, both utterly distinguished: R. P. C. Hanson, sometime Bishop of Clogher, then Professor of Historical Theology in Manchester University, a respected patrologist; George Otto Simms, Bishop of Cork, then of Armagh, finally of Dublin, esteemed as an historian and an authority on the Book of Kells. Three of our priest members became bishops: Joseph Carroll, Auxiliary in Dublin; Donal O'Herlihy, later Rector of the Irish College in Rome, then Bishop of Ferns; William Barden, OP,

Professor in the Dominican theologate, first Catholic Archbishop of Teheran, from which he was expelled because of his friendship with the Anglican bishop.

A list of membership of the Society would include: public servants; Desmond Fitzgerald, former Minister for Defence in the Irish government; F. H. Boland, future president of the United Nations Assembly; W. Fay, future ambassador to France; Joe Walshe, then Secretary (i.e. head) of the Department of External Affairs; writers E. Leen CSSp, A. Doolin OP, Leon Ó Broin, John Betjeman (future poet laureate, then at the British Embassy in Dublin) and his wife Penelope; artists Thomas McGreevy, Mainie Jelett; clergymen from the different Christian communions; leading Catholics in the lay apostolate like Lonan Murphy, president of the St Vincent de Paul Society and his sister Maureen, senior in the almoner service. This was the first continuous dialogue between representatives of the different Christian communions in Ireland since the Reformation. It was one of the most distinguished inter-faith groups ever to assemble in these islands.

The Pillar of Fire Society for dialogue with Jews was also unique of its kind. The membership was less numerous, but not lacking in distinction. Frank Duff and Leon Ó Broin were there, Desmond Fitzgerald also; on the Jewish side we had the entire Jewish Representative Council and many Dublin Jews eminent in their professions. Outstanding among these was Dr Bethel Solomons, probably the most distinguished member of the Jewish community in Ireland. On the Catholic side I should also mention Gabriel Fallon, writer and theatre critic, with whom came his Jewish friend, Larry Elyan, civil servant and accomplished actor.

VII

Both societies were decades before their time, which is not the justification for their suppression. The Archbishop was initially favourable to the Mercier Society. He asked Fr Leen to act as his representative, in a role like that of chaplain. He changed his mind before long and Fr Leen was disconcerted to find that two younger priests, professors in the Clonliffe diocesan seminary, were appointed by the Archbishop to attend meetings and report to him. In addition, certain zealous laypeople took it on themselves to report to him regularly on the meetings; vigilantes of a kind. We identified some of them, and one night when one of our members was speaking as a vigilante zealously transcribed near him, he paused, turned to her and said 'comma'.

Dr McQuaid felt obliged to seek a directive from Rome on a justifiable mode of continuing the Mercier Society. The conditions laid down were, with one expectation, tolerable. This one condition was that the Protestants should not be allowed to defend their positions. How then was dialogue to be conducted?

The voice from Rome was that of Mgr (later Cardinal) Ottaviani, then head of the Holy Office, the man who once described his role and that of his associates as the policemen (*carabinieri*) of the Holy Church – a contradiction in terms to a believer in Jesus Christ and his gospel, at best a sick joke, but not even that to those who, like myself, have suffered from this Roman body.

Dr McQuaid suppressed the Mercier Society. The Protestant committee thought for a while of appealing to Rome, but were discouraged from this by their Catholic friends. Leon Ó Broin and I had a meeting with some members of the Pillar of Fire Society, which was also dissolved by episcopal decree. We could only offer them sympathy. This was tragic. The Jewish people were going through the greatest crisis in their history, the Nazi genocide. I was proud of the fact that our national constitution, sponsored by Mr de Valera, had an explicit mention of the rights of the Jewish congregation. It is the only written constitution which names them; elsewhere they must rely on general freedom of conscience and worship clauses.

We did not then know all the horror of the Holocaust. One night at a meeting of the Society, Victor Waddington, the art dealer, showed us a copy of Victor Gollancz's pamphlet, *Let my People go*, which told on its cover of 300, 000 Jewish deaths. We now know that the reality was twenty times more. The full record to be compiled by a special papal commission will deal with Catholics and anti-semitism: to what extent they may have indirectly favoured the Holocaust. There must also be recognition of the heroic work of Catholics who in the raging storm risked their lives to rescue imperilled Jews. I relate with sadness, almost shame, that we were not allowed to talk to them. I do not regret that I and those with me who were identified with the two societies, the Mercier and the Pillar of Fire, were thereafter suspect. I was doubly so, as I was not only a member of both but the only priest member of the Pillar of Fire. We were fully vindicated by Vatican II. Each of our societies was an exact model of what the Council has prescribed as appropriate means for furthering Christian unity and promoting good Christian-Jewish relations.

VIII

Dr McQuaid was not anti-semitic. His attitude towards Protestants raises more complex problems. Behind his repressive action towards the Mercier Society was the mentality which prompted him to attack Justice Wiley's *Guild of Goodwill*, to support a manoeuvre to oust Protestants from the governing body of a Dublin hospital and to activate the ban on Trinity College. Catholics had been forbidden to attend this university which had a Protestant history, but the prohibition was dormant until he issued a pastoral letter to revive it. The other bishops went along with him. For some years Catholics could enter Trinity only with permission – which was to be obtained from the Archbishop of Dublin! Then the whole anti-Trinity case collapsed; Catholic students are now in a majority. All the time there were excellent Catholics on the teaching body. Alfred O'Rahilly, of whom I shall write later, felt obliged, to the immense sadness of his friends, to defend the Archbishop's policy in the prestigious Jesuit review, *Studies*. He then had a meeting with some of the Catholic lecturers. He told me that he could not hope to find better in the Catholic colleges.

IX

So far I have written of Dr McQuaid from my personal viewpoint. It would be unfair to him to leave it at that. During the decades of his episcopate, institutional progress in Dublin was enormous and, in many ways, very enlightened. Churches were built to meet the needs of an expanding urban population. A large number of religious congregations were allowed or invited to establish houses in the diocese. If the Archbishop had, as we have seen, opposed Justice Wiley's *Guild of Goodwill*, he took positive measures to meet the poverty problem; the Catholic Social Service Conference does vast charitable work in many sections.

Dr McQuaid must get the entire credit for assuring the training of a group of talented priests in radio and television work, the Radharc team. One of them, Fr Joe Dunn, has, in his published work, fully justified this initiative. His team have produced over 350 programmes, a unique audio and television documentary on the church in the modern world – flash points figure, such as the interview with Archbishop Romero three days before he was shot.

The Archbishop established a press secretariat, and began the maintenance of diocesan archives. In a much larger context he advanced the cause of religious education, catechetics, by founding the *Mater Dei Institute*. In another domain he promoted and actively supported Our Lady's Choral Society, which has won praise from people such as Sir John Barbarolli. The Dublin Youth Council dates from his time as archbishop.

Since I have spoken of my personal relations with him, I may be allowed to complete the story which has a happy ending. After a brush with him over a lecture on Pius XII, which I shall deal with, and some queries about pieces I wrote in the *Irish Times* (one was suspect for contributing to this paper), I was to experience great kindness at his hands. After the International Press Congress in Berlin in 1968 which I attended, the incoming Secretary General, Mgr Jesus Irribaren, came to Dublin to seek support for a venue, as he planned the next meeting. Dr McQuaid insisted on my coming with my visitor, and he very graciously offered us tea. There was a minor upset which ended amicably. I thought it better to advise the archbishop who was desirous of helping – though the project was to fail through no fault of his – that there would be Protestant speakers.

A change of temperature. 'Mgr, if you are having a Catholic conference, why do you have to have Protestant lecturers?' The Spanish priest, who had a record of moral courage, went silent. I was now in the firing line: 'What do you think?' 'Well, your Grace, if you want my honest opinion, I would prefer to hear some Protestants speaking about our religion than certain Catholic priests. I would certainly prefer Malcolm Muggeridge to some of them.' Another change of temperature. 'Oh, I would agree with you, Father. Did you read his review in last Sunday's *Observer* of a new history of monasticism? I learned the last sentence by heart, I shall quote it: 'The early monastic founders asked everything of their followers and they got everything; the moderns ask little and they get nothing.'

Soon afterwards the Spiritual Director of the Concilium of the Legion of Mary telephoned me and asked me to become Spiritual Director of a praesidium which was due to begin in Trinity College. Fr Tomás Ó Floinn was very close to the archbishop: he would not have dreamt of making such an appointment without consulting him. The archbishop may even have suggested my name.

These jottings make no pretension to analyse fully a rich, complex character. Dr McQuaid had very remarkable qualities. He was a courageous, uncompromising witness to truths of the faith and of Christian morals. He was a very efficient organiser. His personality summoned loyalty, but some would not pay the extra price. Sadly he accepted flattery too readily, though not all his close collaborators were flatterers. Had he, like Archbishop Mannix, been magnanimous enough to permit dissent in those near to him, he would have had the loyalty of men with high ability and integrity. He was, at times, over-confident in his own judgement and thus blundered in questions like the Mother and Child Act. He lacked the prescience which would have prepared him for the new intuitions of Vatican II, but he showed that he could live with them in practice.

No sketch of him must omit one striking quality and a profound element in his spiritual outlook. He was most approachable to priests 'in trouble' or with personality problems, and this generosity prompted an immense private programme of charity, given to the deserving with discretion and constancy.

There was in his spiritual outlook, part of his innermost fibre, an unbreakable bond, vital and strong, with the Mother of God.

I sometimes think that certain shortcomings in his personality were due to an unusual circumstance in his birth; his mother died immediately after the event. The supreme Mother understood that surely. But she must have been sensitive to all the honour which he gave her, in so many different circumstances of his life. If he found his departure from the episcopal office somewhat trying – 'I have not retired,' he would say, 'I have been retired.' – he had in the exercise of that office, and long before it, accumulated a fund of merit in the sight of Our Lady which stood him well and also eased the final passage. My mention of his name to Pope Paul VI in the course of a brief audience evoked this response from the Pope: 'I venerate Archbishop McQuaid.'

When I sent him a letter of good wishes on his departure from office he replied with a short note thanking me for my loyalty.

9. Monsignor Marcel Lefebvre

I

He was an archbishop, but I shall keep to the French title, Mgr. He was one of the best-known bishops of the post-conciliar era, and to claim acquaintance or friendship with him is like notable name-dropping. However the factual record is all that need concern me.

I was aware that Mgr Lefebvre was a member of my congregation but knew nothing more about him until 1961. He was at the time Archbishop of Dakar. He was due to come to Dublin to attend the Patrician Congress held in June of that year. With another member of the Blackrock College community I was asked to go to the airport to fetch him. He made the same impression on me then as he made many years later when I saw him at Ecône, of which I shall write later: handsome, self-disciplined, courteous, *la suavité même,* as a French journalist once described him, but quite outspoken, amazingly frank in his conversation, and this despite a voice of great softness.

Later in conversation with the Archbishop I noticed something that I was to find over the years characteristic of him. Even in matters where different opinions were tenable and arguable, he was convinced that his view alone was right. He was eventually to show a very high degree of leadership. A constituent of leadership is this certainty in one's opinions. It is therefore important that a leader have the right opinions.

I heard of Mgr from my colleague in the community in the following year. Fr Vincent J. Dinan, though not now superior of our community, had been a representative of the Irish Province at the General Chapter held in Chevilly near Paris that year, 1962. Mgr Lefebvre was not at the time Archbishop of Dakar. He had resigned to hand over the diocese to the man whom he had prepared for it, Bishop (now Cardinal) Hyacinthe Thindoum. Returning to the French hierarchy, Mgr Lefebvre was named to a relatively small diocese, Tulle. The rumour was that John XXIII wished to appoint him to Albi, then vacant, which was ruled by an archbishop; he had a double right to this rank, as he had been Archbishop of Dakar and, as Delegate Apostolic to all French-speaking Africa, he would also have such a title. But the French bishops did not want him in their midst as an archbishop, for this would give him membership of the permanent committee of Cardinals and archbishops, a controlling group in the French church. John XXIII yielded to the pressure.

But now he would no longer be a member of the French hierarchy. Despite hard lobbying against him by some of the French, he was elected Superior General of the congregation. Before long the members realised that they had a new Superior General in more senses than one. This was the pre-conciliar decade when all the forces that would come to a head in Vatican II were gathering. It was, as we can see in retrospect, a golden age in French theology. For some, and these included the newly-elected Superior General, the progressives were getting out of hand and must be restrained. One measure Mgr Lefebvre took to effect this restraint was to disperse most of the teaching staff in the French seminary of the congregation. All but two accepted the decision; these two joined the diocese of Paris, where they were given important posts.

This I know only by hearsay, some years later from one of those affected. I know too that Mgr Lefebvre took a momentous decision. He decided to transfer the Generalate of the congregation from Paris, where it had been for over two hundred and fifty years, to Rome. It was momentous because of the congregation's long involvement with the French colonies, a relationship which even the anti-clerical government of Combes-Waldeck Rousseau had to recognise and respect. French anti-clericalism had waned, if not died, as a result of the two wars: in the first, of the fourteen thousand French priests who were called to the colours, four thousand died; in the second, the French clergy were, in the words of General de Gaulle, the 'very heart of the Resistance'.

To allow the headquarters of our congregation to leave France, without loss of important guarantees in missionary work, the General, now President, had to intervene. On the side of nationalist emotion, Mgr Lefebvre once told my brother, Fr Pat, Provincial in Ireland, that some of his French fellow-countrymen would never forgive him for making the change. The French take a lot of understanding. But they deserve it.

II

In Rome Mgr Lefebvre was soon in the throes of Vatican II. As I was commenting on the debates and decisions for the *Catholic Standard* and *The Leader*, I soon knew where our Superior General stood. I recall a speech which he made in the aula (St Peter's while the Council was in session), opposing the *Declaration on Religious Liberty*. He did not see it coming from genuine Catholic theology, but from eighteenth-century theorists like Montesquieu!

I subsequently learned that this document filled him with alarm, as did the *Pastoral Constitution on the Church in the Modern World*. The idea of collegiality too left him not merely cold but resisting.

Part of Mgr Lefebvre's difficulty with the French hierarchy was the fact that he spoke on his own initiative. They worked as a team and would designate one of their members as a spokesman. Though I differed from him on religious liberty, as I made clear in *The Leader*, and on other conciliar doctrines, I admired his courage. I could not understand the venom some people felt towards him, just on account of his opinions. What is the point of a Council if every viewpoint is not heard?

In time, the intransigent French prelate joined forces with other conservatives to found the *Coetus Internationalis Patrum* which circularised the Council Fathers with material designed to influence their thinking. Another prominent member was Cardinal Michael Browne, OP, the Irish Dominican who had been official theologian to the Pope (Master of the Sacred Palace) and Master General of his order. During the Council, Mgr Lefebvre came to Ireland for the centenary celebrations of Rockwell College, of which the Cardinal was an alumnus. I have a distinct memory of the two men walking around the lake in the beautiful property, in deep conversation. What were they discussing?

The Council ended and we learned that our Superior General had refused to sign two of its documents. Then came the implementation of its decrees. The one that concerned us was that on the *Up-to-date Renewal of Religious Life* (*Perfectae Caritatis*). A General Chapter would be held in 1968, not of the kind previously convened to elect a Superior General and his Council, and listen to hortatory or instructive pronouncements. This was to be a renewal chapter, one to review and, if need be, reform existing rules, constitutions and customs, on the basis of consultation throughout the entire membership of the congregation.

I served on the community commission which surveyed the opinion of its members, on the provincial commission which collated findings from all the communities, and on a commission in the Generalate which aimed at a synthesis of reports from all the Provinces.

Here I met Mgr Lefebvre in the exercise of his office as Superior General. I found him considerate and fair. He came to start the proceedings of our commission, then left so that we should be entirely free. When we returned to our Provinces a group remained on to compile all the documentation needed for the chapter. They too worked unfettered. The results of their work were inspected by an independent expert, who concluded that our chapter was the best prepared of any he had studied.

III

I was elected to represent the Irish Province at the chapter. All in all, it was a traumatic experience and the trauma began on the first day. It centred on Mgr Lefebvre. I must fill in some background. His mandate from the 1962 chapter ran to 1974, but, some months before the chapter, friends and critics had been stunned by the announcement of his resignation effective from the election of a successor during the first session. I know from my close friend, Fr William F. Higgins, one of his General Council and a steadfast friend of his, that some of them tried to dissuade him from this decision. He was adamant.

At our commission meetings in Rome the possibility of making the chapter not only renewal but elective had been discussed; some of the Europeans, French and Dutch especially, wished to see Mgr replaced. Now he seemed to play into their hands. If, as has been suggested, he hoped that the chapter would elect him, thus giving him a lengthier mandate, he nonetheless risked rejection. We heard later that something of a caucus meeting of delegates, Dutch, French, some Irish, had taken place in our Swiss house on the shores of Lake Geneva, at Le Bourveret. It is a good guess that business was mostly Lefebvre.

The crunch came almost at once inside the chapter. The president, a post which was mostly honorary, was the Superior General. But the document describing the structure and the procedure of the chapter itself prescribed that among a number of commissions there should be one central to direct, control and co-ordinate the entire work of the body. The president of this commission should be the Superior General. We had to vote on this and a challenge came from those who feared that Mgr Lefebvre would have too much power over the proceedings. I intervened in the debate and spoke against them. I asked, in particular, what our members in the Provinces and missions would think of us if the first thing we did was to thrust aside (*écarter* was the word I used) our Superior General. Mgr Lefebvre was presiding at the session. He postponed the vote until the next day. Through the delay he may have lost it, for that night there was intense lobbying against him.

When the vote was taken, he lost by 43 to 60. Fr Matt Farrelly,

Secretary General and a stalwart of central administration in Paris and Rome with widespread contacts inside and outside the congregation, has often told me that the figures were as he had calculated beforehand; he knew the thinking of the entire congregation. He himself was loyal to Mgr Lefebvre.

The Superior General left the assembly. He returned once when we had as guest Cardinal Agagianian, head of the Congregation for the Evangelisation of Peoples. My public support for him, which I have never regretted, gave me easy access to him in what was a crisis in his life. He confided in me and discussed different plans passing through his mind. Would he appeal to the Cardinal Prefect of the Congregation for Religious? He could foresee the answer: leave them to themselves and take a holiday elsewhere. Something like that had been the advice given to another Superior General who had a chapter to deal with.

Our Superior General, who construed the action against him as revolt, thought of holding a separate chapter in Assisi with those loyal to him. But it would not be practicable. Out of the days that followed his departure, out of the emotion which he felt and the conversations I had with him, one remark has often come back to me: 'Père O'Carroll, if I have to leave the congregation I shall found a traditionalist seminary and, within three years, I shall have one hundred and fifty students.' Much as I felt for him, much as I admired his integrity and courage, I could not see how this would happen. It seemed to run counter to the overwhelming trend of the time. For in the chapter and in every other centre where Catholics were speaking or writing, the idea of a traditionalist seminary appeared dead. When he died, twenty three years later, he had five major seminaries and had already ordained over two hundred and fifty priests!

IV

On the way there were certainly moments of high tragedy. Mgr Lefebvre's first seminary was founded in Fribourg in Switzerland. Before long he transferred it to Ecône in the Valaisan Alpine region, with his own teaching staff. He went from strength to strength, with demands for seminaries in other countries; one, curiously, was in the region of Castlegandolfo, the Pope's summer residence. Certain religious institutes came under his traditionalist umbrella. Those who looked to him as their spiritual leader, or who thought of him as a guardian of essential doctrine, were numerous.

One reason, complex from the nature of things, which explained this appeal was the sentiment of disarray which many felt, especially in France, in the post-conciliar age. He retained the old Latin Mass, and though he did not think the 'Mass of Paul VI' invalid, he disapproved of it. In contrast with his firm line, many French Catholics saw the innovations, the arbitrary liturgical posturings, do-it-yourself liturgies, as a betrayal. His friend Michel de Saint Pierre, a pacemaker for the Catholic right, a hero of the resistance, has given the factual evidence for all this in two important works, *Les fumées de Satan* and *Le ver est dans le fruit*; the full picture is conveyed in his novels, *Les nouveaux prêtres* and *La passion de l'Abbé Delance*.

Michel is not to be dismissed as a right-wing Catholic with a streak of anti-semitism, as his novel *Je reviendrai sur les ailes de l'aigle* fully demonstrates. I mention him and his works to illustrate a whole climate of opinion that was welcoming to Mgr Lefebvre. He clung to the traditional teaching; he branded as modernism much that was fashionable in Catholic pseudo-theological circles. That he was now a force to be reckoned with was evident from an official visitation of Ecône by two members of the Roman Curia – they were both Belgians. It was evident also in the interrogation to which he was subjected by three Roman Cardinals: Garrone, Wright, Tabera.

Mgr Lefebvre was not locked up in Ecône. He was travelling widely and was everywhere willingly vocal in expounding his ideas and in denouncing doctrinal, pastoral and liturgical errors or misguided practice. From now on he was very much up stage in the Catholic Church. There he got the fullest spotlight possible in the summer of 1976. Against admonitions from Rome he proceeded to ordain priests in Ecône on 29 June, 1976. This to some extent brings him back within my area of observation. I was working in the diocese of Beauvais, and I was a witness to the explosion of interest, excitement and agitation which marked that long, hot ecclesiastical summer. Papers of every hue carried articles constantly about him. In any gathering his name was bound to come up in conversations. *Le Monde*, the intellectual daily, was particularly open to articles expressing opinions about him.

V

Mgr Lefebvre had been suspended from his priestly functions and it was this punishment which vexed certain French people. True, Paul VI had, through correspondence with the Superior General of Ecône, tried to win back the one he thought unfaithful. After the ordination he felt obliged to impose the penalty. When Mgr Lefebvre was asked by a journalist how it affected him, his reply was that he was forbidden to do things which he did not wish to do, that is to perform post-conciliar liturgical acts.

The puzzlement, if not resentment, felt in certain French circles was expressed in the letter sent by eight intellectuals to Pope Paul VI. Asking that the sanction on Mgr Lefebvre be lifted, they pointed to the success of Ecône at a time when French seminaries were in ruin. They sketched a portrait of the church in France which was scarcely flattering:

> For the division is not between Mgr Lefebvre and the other French bishops. It is within the hierarchical church, which allows with impunity the development of so many rites, practices and opinions that we run the risk of seeing shortly as many as there are priests and communities. What marks the church in France at present, and we speak only for France, is the pullulation of these little interior schisms, the proliferation of particular religions. And disobedience to Rome, to the Pope, to the Council breaks out in whatever concerns the liturgy, the priesthood, the training of seminarists and the faith itself.

Contrary to a fairly entrenched opinion that Paul VI would not receive in audience the man whom he had suspended from his priestly functions, without some public act of submission, the Pope received him in Castlegandolfo on 11 September, 1976. At a press conference he told of how he was informed of this. He wrote, as was suggested, a short note asking for the audience; therein he expressed regret if his words had exceeded his thought, and caused pain to his Holiness.

Mgr Lefebvre thought that the result of the audience was positive. He told of one very curious question put to him by the Pope: 'You make your seminarists swear an oath against the Pope?' The reply was categorical: 'Most Holy Father, I am very sorry, but this is absolutely false. Show me this oath, tell me where it is to be found, when I, on the contrary, teach my seminarists respect for the Pope, obedience to the Pope.' A Vatican official denied soon afterwards that the Pope had asked this question. Mgr Lefebvre's comment: 'I'll swear it on a crucifix.'

VI

Some months later I heard that the archbishop would be in Dublin as the guest of the Theology Society of Trinity College. I was invited to speak at the meeting immediately before the one which he would address. I found the students interested and respectful. Now, as to his visit, what was I to do? I sent a letter to the hotel where he was to stay, saying that I would come in to see him the next day. I did so and spent the day with him. At lunch, as I was seated beside him, with Fr Williams (now Bishop Williams) on the other side, he said, placing his hand on mine: 'I said to Father, I wonder will any member of my own congregation come to see me?' In reply I assured him that I could be taken as representing many who were not free.

Our talk ranged over many things. How had the suspension affected his visit to the Pope? 'No one there mentioned it, nor did I.' Did he know that he was being financed by the CIA? – this I had seen hinted at in an English Catholic periodical. He laughed and confessed that when the canard reached him, he had to find out what the CIA was. Likewise in regard to some banks 'linked' with him. Where did he get the money for all his houses? It came, he assured me, in gifts from people not too much endowed with this world's goods. He did not deny, as I had good reason to know, that some of his supporters were very wealthy. But his overall answer was that what he received ultimately came to him through the intercession of the one who has also taken care of his many financial needs in Africa, especially in Dakar, St Joseph.

There was a certain splendour in his unashamed, simple expression of faith in the great devotions of the Catholic faith. He loved Our Lady and trusted absolutely in her power. He honoured Jesus Christ under the sign of his adorable Heart; at a commemoration soon after the Council held in Paray-le-Monial, his secretary, Fr Matt Farrelly, told me that he was the only bishop present.

Apart from a very brief meeting in our Paris house, this was the first opportunity I had to spend some time in his company since the 1968 chapter. As I wrote to an old Irish friend of his, Dr Dan Murphy, next day, I felt that I had been through an experience which left me almost mystified. He was so obviously at peace with himself, and yet how could one justify his position? The fact that I loved and admired him did not remove the enigma. This enigma, and some of his ideas, ideas held very sincerely, meant that it never entered my head to join him. Mgr Lefebvre was magnetic. Two priests, a French Holy Ghost Father, and a Belgian secular priest, each curiously made the same remark to me about him: '*C'est un séducteur*'. Now with the passage of time I think poignantly of what he might have done with this magnetism and his other qualities, had he been able to accept the Council and remain close to the Pope. Frank Duff once told me that he could have saved the entire seminary system in the church. I do know that a priest taking up the post of seminary rector in Rome was advised by Cardinal Garrone to study the Lefebvre seminary – that was at the outset.

VII

Though I did not follow him I was ready to defend him in public and was on each occasion happy to hear expressions of gratitude. I did so in an article accepted by the London *Times*, and for a few minutes, speaking from the audience, in the course of an Irish television programme. One fact about him had to be borne in mind and I did draw attention to it. He was a giant of the African missions. He laboured for thirty years in the 'bush' (his own word) in the senior seminary in Gabon and in Dakar. As well as being bound to the duties of local ordinary (bishop, then archbishop), he was also Delegate Apostolic for all French-speaking Africa. All through his career he was a superb administrator, an administrator thoroughly imbued with idealism.

Mgr Lefebvre came to Dublin again for the blessing of the church which his society had acquired, St John's, Mountown. I think that he was delighted that the blessing took place on St Michael's day. That evening with Fr W. F. Higgins I shared a meal with him in a friend's house. He was brimful of joy, relaxed and, in conversation, expansive. Recalling that John Paul II had received him in audience soon after his election and inauguration, I asked if he would receive Mgr soon again. 'There is a barrier' was his reply (*Il y a un barrage*). There were those in the Vatican not very desirous to have him see the Pope too often. I don't think that they were all non-Frenchmen.

I threw him another sprat and got a salmon: 'I see that Mgr … (French) has gone on holidays with M … (French politician).' 'It doesn't surprise me,' was the reply, 'they probably belong to the same Lodge.'

Fr Higgins and I were saddened some time afterwards to see a worsening of relations between the archbishop and the Pope. Mgr Lefebvre was publicly critical of certain actions of the Pope. He was particularly caustic about the meeting with world religious leaders in Assisi.

We decided to remonstrate with him and Fr Higgins composed a carefully balanced yet respectful letter, which I too signed. Mgr replied with a brief note to say that he was merely adhering to the truths professed by the previous Superior General of the Holy Ghost Congregation, Very Rev Fr Griffin, and others of the same kind.

Then there seemed to be hope of the great reconciliation for which so many hoped and prayed. Negotiations were begun between Mgr Lefebvre and the Roman authorities with a view to an accord that would mean reunion. The negotiations seemed to end in the best result possible for Mgr Lefebvre and his society: the *Fraternity of St Pius X*. The fraternity would have the status of an independent prelature, somewhat like that granted to *Opus Dei*, with at its head a bishop whom Mgr Lefebvre would choose; use of the pre-conciliar breviary and Missal would be authorised; a mixed commission would study points in controversy concerning the teaching of Vatican II. Mgr Lefebvre put his signature to the document which guaranteed these concessions.

Having returned to Ecône, Mgr repudiated his signature. We have been assured that there was no pressure on him from his entourage to do this. It was a moment of heart-break for many of his friends. I did not understand it. It seemed to me then and still does that, had he adhered to his acceptance, his following would have mushroomed overnight. For many who sympathised with his principles and policy and were ready to join him were blocked by his attitude towards Rome, towards the Pope. Once that was cleared up, they would have flocked to him. Jean Guitton, the grand old man of French and European Catholic letters, had described his visit to Ecône in an attempt to dissuade Mgr Lefebvre from consecrating four bishops. This would signal the break with Rome, for he would be excommunicated. Mgr Lefebvre went ahead on 29 June, 1989. His key word that day was: 'I have handed on what I have received.' John Paul II, with a heavy heart I have no doubt, imposed the ultimate penalty. The decree notifying Mgr Lefebvre officially was signed by Cardinal Gantin, a native of Dahomey; he had been named bishop by the former Delegate Apostolic to French-speaking Africa. He expressed his personal grief in a note to the excommunicated prelate.

Some time previously I had visited my friend in Ecône. I was in Switzerland and before leaving Ireland I telephoned him to arrange a visit. When I arrived he had just come in from Italy. He showed me around the seminary which was most impressive, as were the seminarists we met here and there; some were in the chapel, fervent in demeanour. We finally came to the funeral vaults. 'That's where I shall be interred,' he said quite simply. 'Well,' I replied 'we're not surely talking about your death!' 'Père O'Carroll,' was the reply, 'you know that I spent thirty years in Africa.'

VIII

I had another meeting with Mgr Lefebvre. He was in Dublin in October of that same year, 1989, and Fr Daniel Couture, superior of the community attached to St John's church in Dublin, invited Fr Higgins and myself to come and have lunch with them. Mgr Lefebvre was too much a gentleman to remind us, even by gesture, of the letter which we had sent him; when I was in Ecône I never thought of it. But even in the presence of Fr Higgins, who had largely inspired the missive, I did not think of it.

The archbishop was accompanied by two of his volunteer drivers, a Swiss gentleman and his wife. There were people whom he could call on for this service; they seemed to delight in it. They had to drive him from Ecône to the sea and across England to Liverpool where he opened a centre. They would drive him where he wished to go in Ireland, and then take him home.

We were asked to join in a moving ceremony. Fr Couture wished to have the residence consecrated to the Sacred Heart of Jesus. Mgr Lefebvre had been invited to perform the ceremony and we joined in. Then it was adieu.

That was 29 October, 1989. On the morning of 25 March, 1991 I turned on the French radio before going out to say Mass for the Carmelites in Blackrock. I heard the news of Mgr Lefebvre's death and felt a deep pang of sorrow. That afternoon Vassula

Ryden telephoned me to give me the news. She knew of my friendship with Mgr Lefebvre. I told her that I already knew and was trying to make up my mind about going to his funeral. 'If you do, you'll stay here,' she said, which decided me. She lives near Lausanne, not very far from Ecône and, as I left the train and thought of looking for a taxi, a gentleman approached me to say that if I was going to Ecône there was a coach provided by the community. We were passed on the way by a large number of empty coaches coming against us. 'The French came in those,' was the driver's laconic comment. The scene at Ecône was astounding. A gigantic marquee had been erected to hold the immense crowd attending the funeral. There were hundreds of clerics in soutane and surplice; altogether those present may have numbered well over twelve thousand. They came from every country in Europe and from North and South America and Australia. There was a priest from Gabon; Cardinal Thiandoum, retained in Rome, had sent his Chancellor. After the ceremonies in the vast crowd I met some Irish people. Among them was a young barrister, a past pupil of mine, and with him was a retired Admiral of the French fleet. Michael Davies, the Englishman who had written large volumes, *Apologia for Archbishop Lefebvre*, was there but I missed him.

I heard interesting items of news before leaving. Dom Gérard, Abbot of the Benedictine Abbey in Provence Le Barroux, which had been with Mgr Lefebvre and had broken with him in 1988, but on condition that they would not be used to discredit him, had come to pay his respects to his one time leader, as he lay in state. So had the Apostolic Nuncio and the Bishop of Sion, Mgr (now Cardinal) Schwéry; Ecône is in the diocese of Sion.

I later read the account of Mgr Lefebvre's last days. He had been indisposed in the course of a journey from Paris, where he had attended a meeting of his society, and he had been taken to Martigny hospital. He appeared to yield to treatment, but on the night of 24 March, rather into the early morning of the following day, he suddenly worsened and on the arrival of the members of his community, hastily summoned from Ecône, he passed gently away.

He was witty and a spell-binder right to the end. The physician who cared for him was, as his testimony tells, totally captivated by him. He told how the archbishop was confident of the future, speaking highly of his bishops whom he had ordained. At no time had he had any doubt about the rightness of what he had done.

IX

Thus he entered history. What will history say of him? I think that he will be pardoned occasional excesses of language. In life even his friends found this at times trying, but there was so much on the positive side. His doubts about the Council texts are regrettable. His theology of tradition will not be accepted, for tradition moves on, is not, cannot be, immobile. He would argue that there cannot be contradiction between present teaching and doctrine repeatedly affirmed in the past. He had refused to sign two documents, the *Pastoral Constitution on the Church in the Modern World*, and the *Declaration on Religious Liberty*. In the press conference of 15 September, 1976, he intimated that certain others he had signed under moral pressure, but had second thoughts since the Council; this would be true I should think of the *Decree on Ecumenism*. He had been shocked by certain excesses.

Where he impressed many Catholics most was in his respect for the Mass and in his ideals of seminary training. I say respect for the Mass, because I'm not sure that all were drawn primarily to the Tridentine Mass, though here I express my opinion tentatively. I heard a great modern liturgist admit that reverence, which is essential to worship, is often lacking in present day liturgies; obviously it need not be lacking. I do not deny that many of his followers did want the old Mass; this is evident from the fact that in certain areas they were ready to travel so far to get it.

In his celebration of the Mass his strong faith shone through.

I was at first taken aback at a remark by a French friend, a highly cultured person: 'When I see that man say Mass, I know that he has the faith.' On reflection I saw the point. Faith in the priesthood was what decided his ideas and norms in regard to seminary training. It was tragic that John Paul II, who is *par excellence* a Pope of priests, did not have Mgr Lefebvre as an ally.

Pius XII was his Pope. He once said to me that if Piux XII had lived he would have been his first Cardinal from our congregation. I don't think that this was clerical ambition, which I have come across. It was more a statement of fact. It seems true.

If people did not follow all his thinking on the invasion of the church by liberalism, or quite understand why he repeatedly denounced present-day modernism, if they did not reflect on his notion of tradition, they saw him as a priest handling with reverence sacred things, ready at any time to lay his career, his life itself, on the line for God. And with time something like a global fraternity grew around him, each unit deriving strength and assurance from the others.

For this reason he puts questions to the church, as Cardinal Ratzinger said after his death. During his life, Cardinal Hoffner of Cologne had written to him to say that he shared some of his concerns and would like a discussion with him. It took place at length.

His views on church and state may be considered antiquated. Again I do not think that they affected many of his followers. He objected vigorously to the separation of church and state, in which position he belonged to a current of thought that has never disappeared in France. The French Revolution was anathema to those in this tradition, as to him and his family. The last letter preserved in the family archives written by his father, a member of the Resistance who died in a German concentration camp, ended with the words, 'Thank God, I die Catholic and royalist.'

I asked one of our priests, not an admirer of Mgr Lefebvre, a captain in the French army during World War II, how the men practised their religion. In summary his answer was: 'The traditionalists (and they were not my favourites as such) were utterly faithful.' Faith, family, fatherland! As I have said, the French deserve to be understood.

X

When Mgr Lefebvre mentioned Pius XI's Encyclical on Christ the King to one of the Roman visitors to Ecône, arguing from it that Christ as King had rights in civil society, he was shocked to hear the comment: 'He wouldn't write that now.' Hence the title of one of his last books, *Ils l'ont découronné*, 'They have uncrowned him'.

Was he a member of *L'Action française*? I cannot say, but he was in the French seminary in Rome when most of the seminarists were at least intellectually involved – it was even said that some of them used the French weekly for meditation. If any of his family were members I would assume that under the ban of Pius XI, which in retrospect appears very severe in its sanctions, they would have withdrawn. It is not generally known that this ban under which a distinguished French historian, Jacques Bainville, was denied Christian burial, was lifted by Pius XII, when the entire governing committee of *L'Action française* sent him a letter of apology and loyalty. There was a streak of antisemitism in certain members of *L'Action française*. I have never found it in anything that Mgr Lefebvre wrote and he wrote quite a lot.

Interestingly, Mr de Valera was one of Mgr Lefebvre's heroes, and he like to recall that 'Dev' once served his Mass. What impressed him was the uncompromising, public profession of the faith by our president. I do not think that Mgr Lefebvre had read the reference to the Catholic Church in Dev's Constitution. The wording, it has been noted, strongly resembles the formula finally reached in the Napoleonic Concordat. Dev denied any borrowing. Mgr Lefebvre, if he had time to study Constitutional texts would have preferred Franco's declaration in the Concordat of 1953.

10. Pius XII

I

Pius XII was the first Pope whose election was announced at once on radio. His predecessor, Pius XI, had used this medium a few times. We heard the vague sound of his voice on the occasion of the International Eucharistic Congress in Dublin, 1932, when he spoke to those assembled for the final ceremony. Technique was still imperfect and the Pope's voice was not as audible as was that of Count John McCormick, whose *Panis Angelicus* echoed for long in the memories of those who heard him.

Times had changed. Here we were now, a group of seminarists, listening to the announcer from Rome telling us that the man chosen as Pope was Eugenio Cardinal Pacelli, a *Romano di Roma*, first Secretary of State elected for centuries, and in one day, which was his sixty-third birthday, 2 March, 1939. Then we heard the thunderous voice of those assembled in St Peter's Square, those who had been summoned by the white smoke, pouring forth sheer joy in the *Te Deum.* Ten days later we listened to the ceremony of papal inauguration.

The burden of the papacy was on this slender figure, whose name, as Secretary of State, already had magic about it. He was not of the Italian aristocracy but his bearing was that of an aristocrat, one who radiated authentic piety. He was well known outside Italy: as Nuncio in Bavaria and Berlin where he had negotiated the first Concordat between the Vatican and Protestant Prussia; as Papal Legate to the International Eucharistic Congresses in Buenos Aires and Budapest, as Papal Legate to Lourdes on the occasion of a triduum of prayer for peace, in the same capacity in Lisieux for the inauguration of the Basilica which was the world ex-voto to the saint. He had been the first Secretary of State to visit the United States.

The Pontificate of Piux XII was in three phases. First there were the war years, with the deep slide into abysmal horror, the Nazi campaign of genocide and the wanton slaughter of hundreds of thousands of innocent civilians by the Allies in Dresden, Hiroshima and Nagasaki. Then there was the uncertain period when the wartime alliance against Germany split, leaving a perilous vacuum in which Stalin, having shed his bonhomie, stood revealed as a stark, ruthless, marxist imperialist; and finally the grudging acceptance of a status quo in which Russia tightened its grip on eastern Europe and the west consolidated its defensive resources.

In the six months between the papal election and the outbreak of war, the Pope worked assiduously on behalf of peace. His motto was *Opus justitiae pax.* A memorable phrase from those days, 'Nothing is lost by peace – all may be lost by war.' He was head of a sovereign state; as spiritual ruler of the Catholic Church he had subjects in all the countries threatened by a possible war. When Mussolini, convinced that Hitler was unbeatable, made the lunatic decision to enter the war ('an opportunity that comes once in 5,000 years,' he told his son-in-law, Ciano), Vatican neutrality acquired a meaning. If the Duce had listened to the Pope's emissary who tried to dissuade him, Italy's fortune was made. It would not only have escaped the physical destruction caused by modern war, but would have been free of the horrible stain of anti-semitism. After the war, he could have assumed the role of honest broker.

With the end of hostilities one nightmare passed, only to be followed by another, possible domination of Europe by communist governments taking orders from Moscow. The dangerous hollow was 1947; the Brussels Treaty, which would assert western Europe's collective will to fight and sketch the means, had not been signed. NATO, which would follow it, was still in the future. The world was confronted with a possible harvest of death, the result of Yalta, the greatest single disaster – if treachery is too strong a word – in the history of international diplomacy. It had been signed in February 1945, and copperfastened at Postdam in April of that year. Roosevelt was a sick man, Truman inexperienced.

But what explains Churchill's action? Was he a prisoner of his own war-time rhetoric, incapable of shaking himself free from Stalin's grip? How could he hand over Poland to the worst tyrant in history, having gone to war to liberate it from Hitler? Did he not know how Stalin had treated the Warsaw insurgents, halting the oncoming Russian units until the Poles were crushed by the Germans? Churchill ends his account of Warsaw'a agony with the lame comment: 'This cannot be the end of the story.' He also prints the text of the telegrams sent out by the women of the beleagured capital. When he made his 'Iron Curtain' speech in Fulton, Missouri, two years later, a sardonic remark would have been permissible. He had spoken of Hitler and his acolytes sowing the wind, adding 'let them reap the whirlwind'. Who was reaping the whirlwind?

One of the telegrams sent by the Polish women was addressed to Pius XII. His problem now was the fate of western Europe. Stalin did not mount a direct offensive on western Europe, probably because he feared that Russia might be exposed to an atomic bomb. He relied on the French and Italian communists to effect the change he desired. Each failed in its attempt. The general strike planned in France for autumn 1947 collapsed; the Italian communists failed to gain power in April of the following year. Throughout, the Pope had been a powerful symbol of stability, which is not to see him in a crucially determining role. He helped considerably.

II

It was in 1947 that I saw and met him for the first time. On 7 September I saw him addressing a large audience of men in St Peter's Square, one of the first of its kind; such gatherings, with time and some measure of public tranquility, were to become routine. Then on 16 September I was in a group which he received in Castlegandolfo. When he came into the room I had an unusual feeling. I felt that I was looking at a man with all the weight of the world on his shoulders, a man who had to carry on despite enormous lassitude. I almost felt like rising and calling on everyone to go away and let the man rest. He came around to each one, dealt tactfully with a woman who wanted to get from the Pope the solution to some local difficulty. Three days later I was allowed a few minutes personally with him. I asked his permission to dedicate to him a book which I was writing on St Joseph. He was most gracious but reminded me that I would also need an *Imprimatur*! I left his presence strengthened, encouraged. I needed this for I was not totally approved by the local church authority.

In April 1957 I had an opportunity to visit Jordan and Israel. With some friends while in Jordan I went to Amman and found myself inside the royal palace with a number of Americans. King Hussein came into the room where we had been placed, and spoke to us. Apart from finding myself beside ex-king Humberto of Italy in a Portuguese church one Eastertide, it was my only encounter with royalty. Hussein had a reputation for bravery, so I was not at all surprised to note the gentleness and simplicity of his demeanour and bearing. I had reached this conclusion after some study of human courage and had it confirmed by one with experience, repeatedly so with the passage of time. The king spoke quietly in excellent English – he had been to Sandhurst, which saved his life for when he was standing beside his grandfather, King Abdullah, outside the Al-Aqsa Mosque on a day in 1948, the bullet meant for him glanced off a button in his uniform. Abdullah was killed.

I crossed to Israel by the Mandelbaum gate, keeping my book on St Joseph hidden until I was safely there. Thanks to membership of the Pillar of Fire Society, I had from a Dublin Jewish friend, Dr Bethel Solomons, a letter of introduction to the Israeli Chief Rabbi, Dr Isaac Halevi Herzog. I was invited to his residence and while he was receiving Passover visits from his faithful, Mrs Herzog took me aside and said: 'While you're waiting I'll make you a nice cup of Dublin tea.'

Dr Herzog had been Chief Rabbi in Ireland before coming to Jerusalem; he came to Dublin from Belfast. His two sons, one of whom, Chaim, would be president of Israel, received their secondary education in a Dublin school, Wesley College. With us that evening was a great Jewish jurist, Leo Joseph Kohn, who was delighted to meet someone from Dublin. He was the author of a doctoral dissertation on the first Constitution of the Irish Free State, enacted in 1922, and had many memories of Dublin and the National University.

But I seem to have strayed from Pius XII. Not altogether. I spoke of him to Dr Herzog, who surely was a true representative of his people. The Rabbi became enthusiastic. He recalled with gratitude that he had received in a special audience by Pius, exceptionally on a Sunday morning, an audience which lasted a half hour. They had discussed the prophet Ezechiel. When I said that passing through Rome on the way home I hoped to have an audience with the Pope, the saintly old man said with great feeling: 'My blessing to him.'

I did have my audience on 1 May, feast of St Joseph the Worker, a liturgical innovation made by Pius himself. St Peter's Basilica was crowded with an Italian association of workers. Given a place in the circle near the Pope, I had a few words with him as he moved around. I presented to him my little book on St Joseph, and was photographed in the act. The inscription read: 'These pages are offered to His Holiness Pope Pius XII to commemorate his charity to the stricken Jews of Europe.' I also gave the Pope Rabbi Herzog's message, adding that I thought Jews were very grateful for what he had done for them. 'I wish I could have done more,' was his reply. We spoke in French and his exact words were *'J'aurais voulu faire davantage.'* I left St Peter's exultant, not least because of Pius XII's very healthy appearance, a sharp contrast with the impression of fatigue ten years previously. His face was a little plump, but had not lost its classic line.

III

Pius XII was then in his eighty-second year. He had survived illness in 1954, and had resumed at the same tempo and with the rich output, a characteristic activity of what I call his third phase, from the year 1947 when the shadow of a Russian take-over of Europe was lifted. This activity was the delivery several times a week of formal addresses to specialist audiences. Rome was, during those years, a principal congress centre, and those attending these congresses invariably requested an audience with the Pope, knowing that he would speak to them on their own subject in the contemporary idiom.

The papal addresses were fully reproduced in periodical publications called into existence for this very purpose. The range of themes was phenomenal, covering the human and historical sciences, jurisprudence, a wide variety of vocational interests, science in the strict modern sense, cosmology, astronomy, etc. Some people were just dazed by the flow of apparently expert knowledge.

Later when it became fashionable to criticise Pius XII, this aspect of his career was the butt of some cynical comment. I have never seen reasonable criticism of any of the ideas he expressed. It is, I think, certain that he was able to thrust the Papacy and therefore the Catholic thing into a worldwide consciousness where otherwise it would have no entry. How much he relied on research by others has not been revealed; he could not undertake it all, but he had to direct and assimilate the findings, and take final responsibility for the public statement. I came to the conclusion that he had received some enlargement of his mental powers; his capacity for work was clearly beyond the normal; the light in his room was the last to go out at night or in the early morning.

Some years after the Pope's death I was given an interview by Cardinal Tardini, his close collaborator – I was preparing some radio talks on the forthcoming Council. He talked very frankly about Pius XII, whom he admired but did not deify. On the question at issue here he could not give me much information, beyond saying that the Pope's education had been wide-ranging. I have occasionally compared Pius with the other intellectual, John Paul II.

Captivated by the Pope, I felt his death, like many others, as a profound personal loss. I recall vividly the last moments, listening anxiously to the radio reports, late into the night of 8 October 1958, and the shock next morning when I heard that he was dead, the terrible sense of void. The Sunday before he died I had contributed to the *Sunday Times* a piece on him in a series of profiles then running in that paper. My friend Frank McManus, the novelist, then with Radio Eireann, had read it; he asked me to prepare a talk on the dead Pontiff. I assuaged my sorrow by many other journalistic pieces, in the *Catholic Standard* and *The Leader* especially.

IV

The curtain had come down on a mighty career which had marked me, as it did so many others. Henceforth we could ponder his meaning and his message in calm, unruffled by debate or contentious rivalry. He belonged to the ages and we could assign him a worthy place in the sacred pantheon of God's elect. Little did we foresee the intellectual turmoil that would soon surround his memory. Little did I foresee how much I would have to labour for the defence of his good name.

It began with the appearance in a Berlin theatre in 1964 of a play by Rolf Hochhuth entitled *Der Stellvertreter*, produced by Erwin Piscator, a prestigious figure in that world. The theme was Pius XII's responsibility for the Jewish massacre through his refusal to publish an explicit condemnation. The play, put together with skill, was a propaganda piece, made immensely plausible by an instruction which seemed based on sources and by total silence on Pius XII's gigantic relief and rescue operation to save Jewish lives.

Why did the play have such effect, not only in Germany but

in many other countries where it appeared in translation? Why was the author listened to with respect when another play from his pen, implying that Churchill was involved in the death of the Polish wartime general, Sikorski, was dismissed out of hand? He was torn apart in a BBC interview.

A number of factors combined to produce a different effect from Hochhuth's play on Pius XII. There was the shock to many people of first full knowledge of the holocaust, which was followed by a search for the cause. Here was a simple answer. There was the sudden readiness of Catholics to join in criticism of their Pope, a consequence of the loosening of solidarity which followed the Council, sometimes with pitiable results. Catholics felt free to make statements without any appropriate warrant in evidence; the liberal Catholic was henceforth with us and could show the newly acquired freedom by turning on a revered figure in the church.

I have dealt with the essential questions in my book on Pius XII. Before writing it I was involved in one of the longest correspondences to appear in the columns of the *Irish Times*. I published in the paper an article stating in general terms the case for Pius XII. I was soon opposed by a well-known Dublin controversialist, Owen Sheehy-Skeffington, lecturer in French in Trinity College, and son of one of the martyrs of the Easter Week Rising.

Owen and I carried on a running controversy for weeks, digging for material as best we could, neither of us willing to yield or surrender. Some of the letters took up columns. In the end people were naturally bored. I felt isolated, and some Catholic friends were not exactly supportive. One, Seamus Grace, a man of great culture, was utterly staunch and helpful. As to my opponent I felt no particular animosity, and accepted some time later an invitation from the editor of the *Irish Times*, Douglas Gageby, to lunch with him – it could not take place.

There was one immediate sequel to the whole correspondence, another long-term. Immediately Professor Theodore Moody, of the History Department in Trinity College, whom I knew through Leon O'Broin, asked me to help him find someone who would speak on the controversy to the History Society – understandably university students everywhere were fascinated by the topic. I could not find a speaker. I then felt it was my personal responsibility to give the lecture and, of course, face the music, knowing that my opponent would be there and could possibly count on local support.

There was a difficulty. Catholic priests, as I knew from another experience, were not allowed to appear in Trinity. The Laurentian Society, of which I was a member, had to meet outside the university, since the members were Catholic students there. The officials of the History Society agreed to keep silence on my promised appearance. But it leaked and was given some publicity. This involved me in difficulties with the ordinary of the diocese of Dublin.

So here I was on a limb. Entering the lions' den and disavowed, possibly awaiting sanctions from the church representative, the church whose Pope I was defending. It all passed off inside Trinity very amicably. Owen could not appear, as he had had a heart attack that day. The students were gracious. They may have realised that I was the first Catholic priest to speak at a public meeting in the college since it was founded. But, as I remember very vividly, I walked out of the institution lonely and yet intensely happy. I knew there would be some trouble and there was. I felt that on that 8 December, Our Lady's day, powers above would help me. I had only for a short while endured what saints have had to endure for years, the loneliness of being right, of defending the truth but being inconvenient to the very people who should overwhelmingly support you.

V

The long-term result of my private war with Owen Sheehy-Skeffington was the decision to research fully the controversial aspects of Pius XII's career. I had an opportunity soon afterwards of working in the Library of Congress and the National Archives in Washington. I unearthed a great deal of material and this, with what was available in the Vatican War Documents, enabled me to compose a full-scale work on Pius XII. I also used the Nuremberg transcript, that is the record of the evidence tendered at the trials of the German political and military leaders. I learned at the National Archives that there were 16,000 documents prepared but not submitted. I had the constant advice of one of the editors of the Vatican War Documents, Fr Robert Graham, SJ, a prince among scholars. He is the only one I have ever met who was prepared to hand over to another writer the result of his own individual labours.

I cannot reproduce large passages from my book which I have to recommend. No one has challenged my documentation or my conclusions. I know that there were, possibly are, Catholics seriously concerned about the Pope's policy. They are unknowingly the victims of the worst campaign of falsification and disinformation in modern historiography. Let me mention some points which will cause surprise.

The Allies, by declaring and conducting war, had put Jews within the German controlled territory at mortal risk. Hitler had announced that 'in the event of the war's proving inevitable, the Jew would disappear from Europe'. Behind that statement is his ineradicable conviction, his thought-out doctrine that the Jew is the source of every social and political evil, that only extermination would rid the world of this menace. When the war was on, he was goaded to act at once. He used appalling language to an interviewer: should he, having exposed the flower of German youth to death, spare those whom he considered 'vermin' (his word)?

Would a word from a religious leader, whose subjects he had tormented, persecuted, killed in thousands, force him to shed the innermost fibre of his political being? I invite the reader in any doubt to obtain and read what the Führer said about Jews *before* the war. Here was his chance. This was where he could accomplish his mission, which he saw as God-given.

Hence the big question dodged for a long time. What did the Allies do? Nothing, absolutely nothing to save Jewish lives. One elementary means to achieve this end, as I have maintained since I entered this controversy, was to isolate the death-camps, and especially to bomb the railway line to Auschwitz. In the second edition of my book the reader will see the evidence for abysmal failure in this matter. Martin Gilbert, Churchill's biographer, in his book *Auschwitz and the Allies* (London, 1981) reveals that Churchill's approval of a bombing scheme was 'scotched' by a few individuals; it would have meant endangering valuable allied lives (p. 341). Churchill in a message to his Foreign Secretary (11 July 1944) wrote of the crime against the Jews as 'probably the greatest and most horrible ever committed in the whole history of mankind' (*The Second World War*, VI, p. 597).

But what did Churchill do to save the victims? He promised punishment of the criminals after the war. What did Pius XII do? Did he issue a flaming condemnation? Instead he helped save 860,000 Jewish lives. This is the figure given by Pinhas Lapide in his book, *The Last Three Popes and the Jews* (London, 1967). David Herstig in his book *Die Rettung* (Stuttgart, 1967) said at that time there were 360,000 Romanian Jews alone living in Israel who owed their lives to the Pope. These authors are Jews. I have met and talked over the problem with Pinhas Lapide.

I had a brief moment with Jeno Levai, the first and greatest historian of the Holocaust. He repudiated Hochhuth totally. He knew that all Pius would achieve by a public condemnation was retaliation. But could this happen? Holland is the answer. There the Dutch bishops issued a public protest which resulted in a further round-up in which Jews turned Catholics were taken. One was Sister Mary Benedicta of the Holy Cross, Edith Stein. We know from Sister Pascalina, Pius XII's housekeeper, that when the Pope heard of the Dutch disaster he tore up a text which he had prepared, saying: 'If the Dutch bishops' letter cost 40,000 lives, mine would cost 200,000.'

Nearby Belgium had seen a different policy, with admittedly a humane general Von Falkensen to deal with. There was no public condemnation; Jewish money, 3,000,000 francs, stood in the Cardinal's name in a bank; refuge was available to Jews; the

Bishop of Liège had the Rabbi as his secretary. Result: Belgium, 73 per cent of Jews saved; Holland, 79 per cent put to death.

But, agreeing that public protests risked lives and for this reason were deplored by prisoners, was there before the war any explicit condemnation of Nazi horrors? Ribbentrop will give the answer. At Nuremberg he stated, 'We had a deskful of protests from the Vatican.' Another official, Steengracht von Moyland, explained that all deferred to Hitler's known will: ignore them. Altogether Cardinal Pacelli, future Pope, sent sixty-nine protests to the German Foreign Ministry. One of these, a 15,000 word indictment, was so blunt and detailed that it was used in evidence at Nuremberg. Piux XI and Pacelli had, with the agreement of the German bishops, signed a Concordat with Hitler's government to provide legal basis for such protests. When all other efforts failed, the Pope issued the Encyclical *Mit Brennender Sorge,* in 1937. It was drafted by Pacelli with help from the German Cardinals, a condemnatory pronouncement in regard to Nazi theory and practice.

I have maintained and still do so, that Pius XII is the greatest benefactor of the Jewish race in modern times, as John Paul II is the greatest papal benefactor of the State of Israel.

My readers may have the recent sensational news revealed in British State Papers now released. These were given much publicity some months ago in the *Washington Post,* and later in the British media. They show that already in 1941 the British government was fully informed about the massacre of Jews, through interception of German messages and breaking of the codes which transmitted them. It was decided to hush the matter up, for the Germans must not know that their codes were being broken! One State Paper made it clear that they must adopt this policy to avoid the possibility of having to deal with 'wailing Jews'!

Let the Jews be massacred for we must keep our code breakers secret! Will anyone have the gall now to impugn the honour of Pius XII with the knowledge of a government ready to condone genocide? It is no wonder that Jews have been deeply disturbed by the content of these documents. They rightly call for the immediate release of all State Papers relevant to the Holocaust. The truth is great and will prevail. We cannot now be prevented from knowledge of those really responsible for the most appalling crime in the history of a century loaded with crime. Those who have visited Auschwitz, as I have (as I have met survivors), will not be satisfied with anything less than the whole truth.

VI

So much can be concluded from research on the primary sources, the first duty of a historian, and consultation of authoritative works, if possible with their authors – all of which I have done. But have we any evidence of the reaction from contemporary Jews? The answer is in one word: abundant. The Chief Rabbi of Rome during the horror, Isreal Zolli, in gratitude to Pius XII became a Catholic and took as his baptismal name, the Pope's name, Eugenio. He knew that when a ransom in kilos of gold for Jewish lives in Rome was demanded, it was Pius XII who met the demand: the gold was taken and the agreement broken.

Dr Bethel Solomons, whom I have mentioned, told me that he, as president of the Irish College of Surgeons, personally thanked the Pope for his action on behalf of the Jews. The World Jewish Congress voted two million lire to the Vatican in recognition of the Pope's rescue and relief work on behalf of their people. The Israeli Symphony Orchestra, on their first tour in Europe, gave a performance in the Vatican in honour of Pius XII: Beethoven's Ninth Symphony. One could add to the list of those who expressed gratitude.

Whereupon an important question arises: Why do people not accept the findings of Jewish historians on a matter which concerns their people? Does one refuse to accept the judgement of English historians on any of the crises in English history, or of French authors on the French Revolution? Does one reject all the works of Irish historians on the Great Famine? I regard the Jews as the most intelligent of peoples: their record bears this out. Am I asked to believe that, in dealing with the most appalling crisis in their history, they were incapable of discovering the truth? What the question implies is sheer nonsense. They know the full truth.

Then why have those working in the media, with which I include popular drama, chosen to ignore them completely, and sought to explain the Holocaust solely in relation to Pius XII? Why have popularisers of history, contributors to encyclopedias included, repeated the charge that the Pope failed in his duty to the victims because he did not issue a public condemnation? You may find Catholics among those putting forward this idea.

Searching for causes in history is not always easy. I suggest that one should consider such factors as the following: Truth, it has been said, is the first casualty in war. Sometimes morality follows soon after it. The loss, for one and the other, will be to the benefit of the interested belligerent. Those who owe their freedom from the Nazi threat to the Allied Powers are reluctant, even unwilling, to see any defect in those who saved them.

The Allied Powers put the Jewish population of Europe at the mercy of Hitler, not intentionally but as a consequence of his initial victories. They had a moral responsibility to the Jews. This they shirked totally. They did nothing, repeat nothing, to save Jewish lives. What was worse, they effectively condoned, if connived is too strong a word, the massacre by imposing a curtain of silence on the tragic events.

Talk about Pius XII, plays and television programmes about him, conveniently keeps the spotlight off those who were guilty of such a monstrous dereliction of duty. Which leads me to another reflection. The word anti-semitism has, in the light of the Holocaust, such a terrible connotation that one hesitates to use it of anyone other than the perpetrators of this iniquity. But it implies a less than proper idea of the great Jewish people. Are those who put on programmes about Pius XII and the Jews profoundly interested in the race? Are they using them, even using their appalling tragedy, as a vehicle for their denigration of a great Pope?

There is another question, the answer to which again implies such disregard for the Jewish people as would amount to a form of anti-semitism. Do all those involved in the anti-Pius campaign think that they know more about Jewish history than highly qualified scholarly Jewish historians? Have they even heard, have they shown the slightest interest in hearing, of Jeno Levai, the first great authority on the massacre, and the only Jew living abroad called to testify in the Eichmann trial? Would they deal with any other important contemporary problem with such cavalier contempt for the essential witnesses? Do they know that Jeno Levai's book in defence of the Pope was entitled in its German edition, *The Pope was not silent,* and that this title was changed in the English version to *The Hungarian Jews and the Pope*? Do they know that this giant among historians spoke as a witness in the trial of the surviving Auschwitz personnel in 1964, repudiating totally the thesis in Hochhuth's play?

One does not accept the saying of the cynic: 'History is the lie agreed upon.' In the case of Pius XII and the Jews it has some relevance.

VII

I cannot complete my tribute to the great Pope without recalling his immense role as an innovator in Catholic teaching and practice. In this context it is significant that, apart from Sacred Scripture, he is referred to more frequently than any other author in the Documents of Vatican II, two hundred times in all. His encyclical on Sacred Scripture, *Divino Afflante Spiritu*, earned this tribute: *The Jerome Biblical Commentary*, joint work of great American biblical scholars, carries this dedication: 'To the memory of Pius XII whose promotion of biblical studies bore fruit in the Vatican Council.'

The Rights of Man. The Popes tended to avoid this phrase because of its association with the French Revolution. To John XXIII is given the credit of showing that the rights of man are not only compatible with the faith but amply supported by it. John XXIII was not the pioneer in this valuable development: it was Pius XII who proclaimed the doctrine, listing the principal human rights, in his 1942 Christmas address. John makes this quite clear in his encyclical *Pacem in Terris.* Altogether he refers thirty-three times to Pius XII's writings, eleven times to this single Christmas address.

To anyone working on Marian theology as I was, it was a joy to have in Pius XII a Pope who presided over a true Marian age. He consecrated the world to the Immaculate Heart of Mary in 1942 and Russia, in an encyclical, ten years later, the only such papal document addressed directly to the Russian people. In 1950 Pius solemnly defined the dogma of the Assumption; four years later he proclaimed the universal queenship of Mary; he declared two Marian years, one for the centenary of the dogma of the Immaculate Conception, 1953/54, the other for the centenary of the Lourdes apparitions, 1957/58. The Pope gave encouragement to theological study of the mystery of Mary, as he supported associations like the Legion of Mary. Fittingly, his last broadcast to a Marian assembly was on 17 September 1958, three weeks before he died on 9 October 1958. His words, spoken then to the Marian Congress in Lourdes, at which I was present, are treasured by people like me who believe that he will be canonised and declared a Doctor of the Universal Church. His words that day: 'I wish to state, at the conclusion of this congress which crowns this incomparable Marian year, my unshakeable conviction that *the reign of Jesus will come through the reign of Mary.*'

11. Frank Duff

I

I have met briefly in life a number of people who may one day be canonised. One who may be so honoured by the Catholic Church, Frank Duff, I knew very well. I saw him in all his moods and tenses for more than four decades. I met him for the first time in the central office of the Legion of Mary, which he founded, in 1937. I attended a meeting of the Pauline Circle, an inter-faith group, where he spoke – and with some vigour– three days before he died. It was Tuesday 4 November 1980. His death was to occur on Friday the seventh. St Augustine, who loved interpreting numbers, would have delayed on the importance of '7' in Frank's case. He was born on 7 June 1889; he founded the Legion of Mary on 7 September 1921.

He had a long life, but I am in a position to testify that his mental powers were unimpaired to the very end. In that last encounter he was just the same Frank I had always known. There was a black mark on his forehead which, he told me, would be treated. His friend, Dr Michael McGuinness, present that night, later told me that it was a rodent ulcer. It mattered little to Frank. One of his great relaxations was long-distance cycling, and he had planned the intinerary – around the Head of Howth, at the end of Dublin Bay – for the following weekend.

Death came to claim him, offering a different itinerary. There was little delay in the call or the response. That morning he had, in addition to his daily Mass, attended a Requiem Mass for the Legionary Envoy, Joan Cronin – her areas had been Latin America and the Middle East. Frank was delighted to receive Holy Communion twice. Returning from the graveside to the

Regina Coeli Hostel, he was disinclined to eat and decided to rest. He forbade the Hostel sister attending him to call a doctor. Some hours later she went to see him hoping to suggest a cup of tea.

Frank was dead. His hands were folded on his breast as he lay on his bed. Nearby was a copy of Cruden's Biblical Concordance; he had apparently been preparing a lecture. For a man aged ninety-one years and five months, this was a splendid exit; for one who had twice within the previous few years been physically assaulted by hoodlums who broke into his residence, in one case leading to a stay in hospital, it represented a special triumph. It was the sealing of a legend.

Frank Duff did have his legend. Intrinsic to it was exceptional vitality. His family background would be middle class, middle class in the context of an Ireland governed from Westminster, with all that this entailed. Practice of the Catholic religion was free, but many of the social and economic levers were still in Protestant hands; but not education. Catholic teachers staffed the National Schools at the primary level. Catholic secondary schools existed through the initiative of religious congregations of priests and sisters and brothers; a number of these congregations had come from the continent.

II

The future Legionary founder was sent to Blackrock College, located in the Dublin suburbs. It had been founded in 1860 by a group of French Holy Ghost Fathers, led by a remarkable religious who was destined to become a foremost educationalist in the country of his adoption, Fr Jules Leman. French priests were still in the College in the days of Frank's schooling, and the religious atmosphere and training owed much to French tradition. Frank retained a very vivid memory of the preparation given to those who were to receive their First Communion.

Famous men tend to be either backward or brilliant in their schooldays: brilliant, foreshadowing their future achievements; backward, showing that ignorance of the future is the handicap of those who educate men of genius. Frank's record, coldly preserved, shows that he was brilliant. And already he had character. When the family changed from the residence relatively near Blackrock College to the other side of the city, he insisted, despite his mother's wish to send him to a school nearby, on cycling right across Dublin city, morning and evening.

Thereon hangs the first of the *Fioretti* in this interesting life. Cycling so far, the young boy was often late for the first class, and thus incurred the wrath of a teacher who seems to have disliked him. The teacher would invariably send Frank to the Prefect of Studies. In those days of spartan discipline this would generally mean physical, that is corporal, punishment. The priest who was Prefect, Fr James M. Keawell, CSSp, was strict. Surprisingly he made an exception of Frank, and went so far eventually as to move him to a lower class, to a more kindly teacher.

In the national examinations at the year-end Frank got a higher mark than all the boys in the class from which he had been changed. And Fr Keawell received a touching testimony of gratitude. One day after saying a parochial Mass in a church in Bray, some fifteen miles from Dublin, he found Frank waiting for him – he had left school some months previously. He presented to the priest a gold card case purchased with the very first personal income he had earned.

Many years later when Fr Keawell died, Frank came to pay him homage. I had come to know the former Prefect, at one time my teacher of Latin, as a colleague and I made some remark about the loss. I then heard a spontaneous tribute of a kind I had never heard before, or since: 'I had a great sense of triumph up there.' Some time later, at a meeting of the Pillar of Fire Society, I gave the gold card case to Frank. He placed it in my hand and pressed his hand affectionately on it.

The future Legionary founder would, on his examination results, have merited university education. For family reasons he chose to take up work at once. He entered government service, at the time British. With the establishment of the Irish Free state in 1921 it passed to native control. At the moment of the Irish take-over, he acted as secretary to Sir Cornelius Gregg, who worked out and implemented the details of the transition. Gregg launched the Irish Civil Service on a course of efficiency and integrity. Frank admired him. They had been educated at the same Irish school. His work accomplished, he returned to London, where he ended his career as Chairman of the Board of Inland Revenue.

Frank had steady, not spectacular, promotion in the Irish Service. At one time he had responsibility for housing in the city of Dublin. A memorandum which he then prepared was many years later presented by him as a theme for analysis and debate to a discussion group, composed of past students of his old school, the Aurora Society.

III

In the first phase of his life, the battle to carve out a career, there was one determining influence, that of his mother. He had been brought, earlier than is customary, into the family counsels, and there grew up between them a relationship most profound and devoted. She was attentive to his every need, and he kept rigorously to certain filial duties towards her. It was told amusingly by a friend that he would take time off from his crowded work schedule to take her to the cinema once a week. She would enjoy the picture and he would fall asleep. Shortly after her death we had occasion to spend an evening together. As we parted I renewed my sympathy. Then he said simply: 'Now I feel I have nothing left to live for.' He was once asked by one of a group of friends whom he would first look for in heaven. Those aware of his incomparable devotion to Our Lady were surprised to hear his reply: 'My mother.'

She must have taken immense pride in all he accomplished for God and his church, as the years passed. She had, too, moments of special grace. One night as her son was entering their home he was accosted by a down-and-out who pleaded to be given shelter. Frank brought him into the house and gave him his own bed, sleeping on a downstairs couch himself. He left the house in the morning to attend Mass. When he returned for breakfast his mother had a strange query for him: 'Who was the lovely young man who slept in your room last night? I saw him leaving while you were at Mass!'

In the Civil Service Frank made friends with people who would in one way or another help him in the great extra-curricular activities of his life. Sean Leydon, one of the most distinguished government servants in the history of the state, was deeply attached to him, asked him to be best man at his wedding. Sean helped him financially in his expanding programme of social work.

Leon O'Broin was a particularly close and staunch friend then and always. Like Frank he had joined the St Vincent de Paul Society – the Civil Service was its backbone in Dublin in those days. As a boy he had seen Frank in action in the anti-proselytising area. Now having left the National Army, as Ireland's first defence force was called, and moved into the Civil Service, he found himself in the Department of Finance where Frank was his superior. A distinguished historian, he has told in his life of Frank and in his autobiography, *Just Like Yesterday*, something of the lighter side of life within the offices where government servants mostly worked.

IV

Frank Duff never lost his sense of humour. Rather it grew with the years, and Leon O'Broin once remarked to me that our mutual friend found relaxation in the hearty laughter so characteristic of him.

He was soon to carry a work-load which made relaxation indispensable. The first step towards a life of dedication in the lay state had been the decision to join the St Vincent de Paul Society. That was in 1913. Eight years later the Legion of Mary was born. Frank had served a most valuable apprenticeship with the older association. He learned the importance of group decisions and of co-operation in the service of the poor. He learned to share ideas, and he learned the very great value of a precise task assignment, fulfilled within a fixed time, with a report delivered to indicate just what was achieved; he also learned the sound psychology of visitation in pairs.

Legionary meetings, held weekly, were given a more detailed prayer structure than was prescribed for some other lay associations. And there was distinctive idealism. Here again the founder was indebted to the St Vincent de Paul Society. It was a fellow member, the well-known Dublin architect, Vincent Kelly, who gave him a copy of what was to become the book of his life – not that he was a man of one book. It was *True Devotion to the Blessed Virgin Mary* by St (still at the time Blessed) Louis Marie Grignion de Montfort. Frank's first reaction was unfavourable. But he changed his opinion and was, before long, captivated by the Marian theology and sheer spiritual logic of the work.

For this man was an activist, a doer, an achiever. As he had to face one thorny problem after another in his apostolate – the foundation of the *Sancta Maria Hostel* for street girls, the *Morning Star Hostel* for down and out men, the *Regina Coeli Hostel* for unmarried mothers – each bristling with complications, contradictions, nerve-wracking drudgery, he had to have a solid core of idealism. He found it in De Montfort's doctrine of Mary, Mediatress of All Graces. Then he went deeper into the mystery of the Christian life and saw the relevance of the Pauline idea of the Mystical Body of Christ.

Enlightening as it would be to pursue the development of the spiritual doctrine, it would possibly be more helpful to look at some of the features of the association. The Legion of Mary was set on a course of worldwide expansion, to the other centres in Ireland outside Dublin, then to Scotland, to England, to wartime Europe, Australia, North America, Africa, South America, the Far East, the Middle East, and eventually in Frank's lifetime to 1,300 dioceses.

In this worldwide setting members were engaged on a wide diversity of works. They could be asked to do anything that would serve the church, but there was a cast-iron rule: material relief could not be given. The unit of the Legion was the *Praesidium*, true to the general Roman nomenclature. Praesidia existed in very different milieux. Some ran the hostels, *Regina Coeli, Sancta Maria*, and *The Morning Star* .

I made slight contact with the Morning Star. I once gave a day's retreat to the men, one of whom told me that at one time it was not the Morning Star but the Ritz in London! I also heard of the young man who was showing a close interest in the medical care of the residents. The Legionaries in charge found that he was a medical student who had completed his academic course, but because of a 'problem' had not taken the examination. They found out that he was still eligible. So they got him the necessary literature and he got down to study. He passed his finals, the first doctor to graduate from a Legion of Mary hostel!

V

As I have already stated, my first service to the association was as Spiritual Director to a praesidium named *Mater Salvatoris*. The members kept a book barrow in O'Connell Street, Dublin, the main city artery. The idea of the book barrow was not merely to sell Catholic publications. It was a means of personal contact; the need for personal contact was central to Frank Duff's theory of the apostolate. For me it was enlightening to hear the reports given at the weekly meetings by those who had done duty, night after night, on the book barrow.

From *Mater Salvatoris* praesidium, I moved to *Joy of Israel*, whose members worked among the Jewish population. This was the seedbed of the Pillar of Fire Society, of which I have written. I also served as Spiritual Director of a praesidium recruited among Blackrock College past pupils, *Sanctuary of the Holy Spirit*. It was a joy to Frank Duff that praesidia existed among the present and past students of his college.

The suppression of the Mercier and the Pillar of Fire Societies, of which I have written, was a heavy blow to Frank Duff. The action stemmed from a rigid attitude in the Roman Curia in face of the different inter-faith movements which manifested a deep desire in many Christian bodies for unity. I am not concerned here with this reluctance to consider any change, its history or cause. The signs were that change would come. Writers of intellectual substance were addressing the themes relevant to Christian unity. Pius XI's use of the word 'panchristian' to describe the incipient World Council of Churches (*Mortalium Animos*, 6 January 1928) is in marked contrast with the language of an Instruction issued from Rome on 20 December 1949. Now the World Council of Churches was a reality and the movement towards unity which it embodied was not to be explained merely by external events and cultural changes; for it had been awakened 'under the inspiring grace of God'.

All this was in the future at the time of the Mercier Society. Frank Duff would be excused for seeing the official intervention in the line of much that he had been made to endure over the years from clerical hostility. He was sensitive on the point. He had been an innovator. He had shown that the laity could think for themselves. His projects had succeeded. As they did, they stirred some jealousy among the clergy, jealousy that was probably largely unconscious, covered with a veneer of righteousness. It was at times corporate and hardened.

I heard Frank talk of this painful experience more than once. The pressure on him took various forms. I have heard that there was a whispering campaign among the clergy that he was mad and should be avoided. Those with an eye on clerical promotion in the diocese tended to avoid him. One Archbishop of Dublin refused for years to see him, though he was recommended by laymen highly thought of in the diocese like Sir Joseph Glynn, president of the St Vincent de Paul Society and Matthew Lawlor, Dublin area president. Much later, when he was known and esteemed throughout the church, he was subjected to the humiliation of having a new edition of the *Handbook* of the Legion held up for censorship reasons for over a year – incomprehensibly.

VI

I heard Frank tell a small group who were away for a weekend reflection that he had just assisted at the consecration of an Auxiliary Bishop of Dublin. As the procession of senior clerics entered, he asked himself wistfully if he could count on anyone among them as a friend. He told me privately that for years he awoke each morning with a sense of dread: Would he be asked this day to close down the Legion of Mary?

He was a fighter. To a very dear mutual friend he once gave as a Christmas present a copy of Rembrandt's *Knight*, saying 'You know I'm a fighter.' So there were moments when attack was fought off. One day a priest arrived at Legion headquarters to transmit an order from the Archbishop that Sancta Maria Hostel should be closed. 'I must have that in writing. I shall nail it to the door,' replied the Legionary president, 'so that everyone in Dublin will know who is driving the girls back on the streets.' That was the end of that.

Another threat ended similarly. An official from the Department of Local Government arrived one day to announce that since there was nothing in writing authorising possession by the Legion of the house used as the *Sancta Maria* hostel, the Department would have to reclaim it. No notice was taken of Frank's protest that the transfer had been made by Mr Liam T. Cosgrave, head of the government and also Minister for Local Government. No, the house must be taken back by the government. 'Well then,' was the reply, 'prepare yourselves for the greatest eviction scene in Irish history. The Legionaries and the girls will barricade themselves inside. We will use every means possible to defend ourselves and I will be the last one dragged screaming out of the building.' Frank told them that there would be advanced notice to the public, so that a military cordon would be needed to keep spectators at a reasonable distance. End of story.

For Frank's first papal audience it was to Dr Downey, Archbishop of Liverpool, that he applied for a letter of commendation. The audience was granted, 16 September 1936, though he told me that he thought a discreet word had been passed by Mr Cosgrave, now a devoted friend. A senior cleric in the diocese, whom I prefer not to name, was ill-advised enough to remark at a convent luncheon in presence of several priests, 'Well poor Duff has been in Rome looking for an audience, but without success.' Frank called on the prelate and attacked him verbally. Did he have nothing better to do than misrepresenting the faithful of his diocese, and on into full crescendo. The poor man was badly shaken by the storm that hit him. He went immediately to Mr Matthew Lawlor. 'Oh, Mr Duff has been to see me and he said terrible things to me.' 'I agree with every word he said,' was the comfortless response.

If a prophet is without honour in his own country, that honour is often given him in abundance elsewhere. Frank Duff did have friends in his own country. They were true friends, for the friends of those under stress are disinterested. They included priests, many from the religious orders and congregations. Above all, support of a very valuable kind came to the Legionary founder from abroad. People like Fr Emile Neubert, SM, the well-known Marianist writer, would be attracted by his Marian idealism; Cecily Hallack, a prominent English Catholic writer, saw the wide ecclesial and social impact of the association and wrote the first full-length book on it. Some years later, the most important recruit to Legionary crusaders came in the person of Léon-Joseph Suenens, Auxillary of Malines-Brussels, later Cardinal Archbishop of the same See, destined to a very important role in the life of the church. His work on the *Theology of the Apostolate*, a commentary on the lengthy formula of commitment to Legionary service pronounced by a member on the day of his or her induction, was something of a landmark. It was followed by other works related to the association, notably the first full-length life of Edel Quinn, best known among the envoys sent to spread the Legion. It was Cardinal Suenens who urged Pope Paul VI to invite Frank Duff to Vatican II as an Auditor.

VII

The personality of the man at the centre gained in confidence and fulfilment as the organisation grew. The multiplicity of demands tested his nervous and mental energy and his spiritual equilibrium. It all meant long, exhausting hours for he had bound himself to full recitation of the Roman Breviary every day – I once heard him say that he sometimes completed it at four o'clock in the morning when he was 'crazy with fatigue'.

The worldwide growth of the Legion down to the present time, when its expansion in South Korea is phenomenal, invites consideration of the founder's spiritual doctrine.

Where shall we find this doctrine? Principally in the *Handbook of the Legion*, which is more a compendium of spirituality than a set of rules or a summary of structural requisites. It was obligatory reading for members, and contained also the prescribed prayers. Over the years Frank also composed different works setting forth spiritual teaching. At intervals, volumes were issued from Legion headquarters which were collections of occasional addresses and papers. These addresses were given at Legionary meetings of one kind or another; the papers appeared in the official journal, *Maria Legionis*.

How much spiritual advice of general import was conveyed in the founder's correspondence is a matter for conjecture. The extent of this correspondence is incalculable. Frank was a very skilful user of the dictaphone and took to it very soon. I questioned him once on the amount he dictated week by week; I concluded that he was dictating about thirty thousand words annually. This was at a time when letters were reaching him from all over the world and when envoys especially were reporting progress in their regions. Many who corresponded with the founder sought advice which would pass beyond administrative demands. He was, in his replies, optimistic, articulate, always urging a courageous spirit.

I was once asked to give some information about him to American priests preparing a special issue of their religious periodical devoted to him. I had in my possession a volume of his letters, that is of the copies retained. We opened it at random to look at the matter and style. Several letters written to Alfie Lambe, Legionary envoy in Brazil, urged him to examine the possibility of extension to the Falkland Islands. This surprised us, as the Falklands war was being fought at that time.

Those who do not accept Frank Duff's spiritual, theological outlook in all its ramifications as in its essentials, must see it, nonetheless, as a whole. When Mary's universal mediation is mentioned as central to his thinking, an *idée-force* to borrow the French phrase, there may be some misgivings. But he did not have things out of proportion. He was a man of the church and lived by the great certainties of the faith. Before reading him on the subject of Mary's great power with God and her irreplaceable role in our lives, we should ponder such words as these: 'The Legion is built in the first place upon a profound faith in God and in the love he bears his children. He wills to draw great glory from our efforts and he will purify them to render them fruitful and persevering… The Legionaries' essential mainstay must be this knowledge of the companionship of God, their good Father, in their twofold work of sanctifying themselves and serving their neighbour.'

VII

I ask the reader's indulgence for some further quotations, as Frank's own words are convincing. This is what we read a little further on: 'But what is the place of Mary herself in relation to God? It is that he brought her, as he did all the other children of earth, out of nothing; and though he has since then exalted her to a point of 'grace immense and inconceivable', nevertheless in comparison with her Maker, she still remains as nothing. Indeed she is – far more than any other – his creature, because he has wrought more in her than in any other of his creatures.'

In the framework of thought, words like the following should be read: 'For us God has constituted her a special means of grace for she is the Spouse of the Holy Spirit; she is the channel of every grace which Jesus Christ has won. We receive nothing which we do not owe to a positive intervention on her part. She does not content herself with transmitting all, she obtains all for us. Penetrated with belief in this office of Mary, the Legion enjoins it as a special devotion and sets in its Catena, for daily recitation by every member, the proper prayer of the Feast of Mary, Mediatress of all Graces.'

This idea is part of the intellectual fabric of the *Handbook* and recurs frequently in its contents. It is axiomatic in the thought-content of the work, as of the whole association. Frank Duff soon learned, as he became more fully acquainted with the life of the church, that he was in a mighty current of Marian renewal stemming from Belgium. A great national educational and spiritual leader, Désiré-Joseph Cardinal Mercier, had remarkably reversed a sad trend in doctrine about Our Lady and devotion to her.

Things were, in this domain, weak and uninspiring in the first decades of the century. Mercier was, in the post-war years, at the peak of his career. With characteristic courage and zeal, he launched a whole programme of instruction on the message of St Louis Marie Grignion de Montfort, whose book he had read and found totally convincing. He initiated a worldwide movement to have Mary's mediation of all graces declared a dogma of faith. Eventually Pius XI would set up three commissions to study the matter, Belgian, Spanish, Roman.

The year 1921 was a milestone in Mercier's apostolate. In that year he issued his famous pastoral on the theme he had made his own; in that year he organised a congress in Brussels to pool theological thinking; and in that year Rome granted his first request: Pope Benedict XV approved a Mass and Office of Mary, Mediatress of all Graces. It would be granted also to other bishops and to heads of religious institutes who requested it. In that same year, 1921, the Legion of Mary came into being. The growth of the Legion proved the truth of Mary's mediation in practice.

There is a basis of comparison here with the *Militia*

Immaculatae, founded by St Maximilian Kolbe. He was equally explicit in his affirmation of the universal mediation of Mary. In a totally different context, the survival of the Catholic Church in Poland under the leadership of Cardinal Wyzshinski owed much to the unyielding faith of the Cardinal in the same truth.

IX

Along with belief in this truth, Frank had another very strong conviction. This was on the universal vocation to the apostolate. Here he had a clarity of vision which was not shared by many in the church, apart from those to whom he communicated it. Frank did not see the apostolate, that is service of the souls of others, as a means of sanctification, an option among others, like penance, spiritual reading, meditation. It was an essential part of the Christian vocation. To be truly a Christian one must be an apostle. An 'individualistic religion directed exclusively towards the benefitting of one's own soul and not at all concerned with one's fellow-man' he stigmatised thus: 'This is the "half-circle" Christianity so reprobated by Pius XI.' A Christian, Frank once said, must 'pour his soul into another soul'. Or again, 'apostleship and faith constitute the life of the church'.

It will be readily admitted that not many were speaking or writing this language in the days before Vatican II. The Council heavily endorsed Frank's contention: 'For this was the church founded: that by spreading the kingdom of Christ everywhere for the glory of God the Father she might bring all men to share in Christ's saving Redemption; and that through them the whole world might be brought into relationship with him. All activity of the Mystical Body directed to the attainment of this goal is called the apostolate, and the church carries it on in various ways through all her members.'

These words are taken from the *Decree on the Apostolate of the Laity* (no. 2). They are in essence found in parallel passages in other conciliar documents. I cannot say with certainty that the thinking of the Council was directly influenced on the point by Frank Duff. But his thought had permeated over a thousand dioceses in the church. One conciliar passage, which was officially admitted as due to an intervention by Cardinal Suenens in the stages of textual redrafting and amendment, could have been written by him; Cardinal Suenens has never denied his debt to Frank. The words are: 'Hence the church in her apostolic work also rightly looks to her who brought forth Christ, conceived by the Holy Spirit and born of the Virgin, so that through the church Christ may be born and grow in the hearts of the faithful also. The Virgin Mary in her own life lived an example of that maternal love by which all should be fittingly animated who co-operate in the apostolic mission of the church on behalf of the re-birth of men and women.' (*Constitution on the Church*, no. 65)

To reassure the reader I had better quote Cardinal Suenens on this specific point: 'By uniting Mary with the apostolate, the Legion strives not to separate, in its soul and action, what God has united. The Second Vatican Council at my request willed to emphasise this alliance, which is the soul of the Legion of Mary.' The Cardinal adds: 'This conciliar text was, to my knowledge, a joy and comfort to Frank Duff, who appreciated what it said and implied.'

X

Behind this theory was an exceptional if not unique knowledge of the church in our time. Through the envoys, one more splendid than the other in initiative and achievement, through the *Peregrinatio pro Christo* movement (teams of volunteers sent to countries where the Legion needed help or where it did not exist), through the innumerable visits from Catholics of every rank in the church, through the vast correspondence received and despatched during a long life right to the end, this unique individual acquired an in-depth, multidimensional knowledge of Christ's church rarely equalled outside the immediate governing entourage of the Pope. It was knowledge drawn from experience, lived from day to day. It will probably overwhelm whoever undertakes the task of reading Frank Duff's correspondence, about which I have written, of which I estimate the contents at well over a quarter of a million items.

So was it a pragmatic doctrine that inspired the Legionary founder? He knew what was wanted and did his best to meet urgent need, without pondering the reason why. Not at all. Frank had wrestled with the problem of motivation in service of others. He told me that he thought people who found it hard to see Christ in their neighbour would more easily serve him or her as a member of Christ's Mystical Body. The Legionary read in the *Handbook* that his service was based on this doctrine, and this was more than a decade before the Encyclical of Pius XII, *Mystici Corporis Christi*, which sealed and crowned the work of theologians rescuing this capital concept from quasi-oblivion.

Frank Duff's task was to make the Mystical Body an ideal to stir enthusiasm, loyalty, self-sacrifice. He did it, to some extent, by the force of his own spiritual personality. Again and again I have noted how people of character were mentally moulded and morally motivated by him. I never met Edel Quinn, but I would put her in that category. Is this a departure from the theology of the Mystical Body? It is the way that Christ works in his Mystical Body to make it a living truth for his disciples.

It is a truth with many ramifications and many of them this great lay apostle pondered. One is the role of the priest, the minister of Christ in his Mystical Body. Many heard, at the time of the Council, during the fourth session when Frank was a Lay Auditor, of the compliment paid him by Cardinal Heenan, a former spiritual director of the Senatus, that is the highest national governing body of the Legion in England. His Eminence singled out the Legion as a lay association wherein collaboration between priest and laity was admirable. His words were greeted with acclamation.

Frank had, from the early days, an intuition that the Holy Spirit must be central to the idealism of the Legion. The opening words of the formula of personal commitment, the legionary promise, are: 'Most Holy Spirit, I (name of candidate) desiring to be enrolled this day as a Legionary of Mary, yet knowing that of myself I cannot render worthy service, do ask of thee to come upon me and fill me with thyself, so that my poor acts may be sustained by thy power, and become an instrument of thy mighty purposes.' This was, at the time, an innovation. In those days we are not far from the publication of *Le Divin Méconnu* (English translation, *The Forgotten Paraclete*), about the time also when Dom Columba Marmion would begin his retreat lecture on the Holy Spirit by recalling the answer of some neophytes to St Paul's question on whether they had received the Holy Spirit (Acts 19:2). The great Benedictine would say that at present some, if not many, Catholics seemed to be in the same plight.

Note finally that St Louis Marie chose Incarnate Wisdom as the subject of his act of consecration. Frank did not follow him, nor did he choose Our Lady. He wrote in the *Handbook* that the Holy Spirit 'received far too little devotion from the general body of Catholics, for him Legionaries must needs have special love.' He linked this view with his idea of the Mystical Body. He went on in his last years to reflect much on the union between Mary and the Spirit, anticipating the post-conciliar interest in the theme. I had one lengthy conversation with him on the subject and I found it profoundly illuminating. His thinking is contained in some essays, one of which he thought the best 'thing he had written' – his words to his god-child, the economist, Finola Kennedy, herself author of a penetrating study on *Frank Duff and Newman*.

XI

The legacy of Frank Duff is, therefore, rich and manifold, attached at deep truly valid points to the life and tradition of the church. For me it is a legacy happily linked with mutual friendships, notably with all that the name Leon O'Broin evokes in my memory. I dedicated my first book, *This Age and Mary* (Cork, 1946) to them both. Leon lived on for almost a decade after Frank. His last years were passed in different nursing homes, with illness which he bore with exemplary patience.

Leon had been a force in his time. He was at the peak of his power and the summit of his career in the fifties. He had been closely associated with Frank in the Civil Service and in the

Legion of Mary. He was prominent in the Irish language movement, had access to the Dublin theatrical world, then rejoicing in a number of rich personalities – did someone say that no matter what happened there would be Irishmen writing plays and Russians playing chess? Leon was a writer, as yet mostly in Irish, and he was trusted by the writing community in Dublin; this too was not lacking people who shone, as well, of course, as those who merely sparkled. He was able to induce some of the committed Catholics, Frank McManus, the novelist and Roibeárd Ó Faracháin, the poet, to take an interest in the Legion.

Leon, in his autobiography, has told the story of a third society founded on an initiative taken by Frank, himself and writers who had met them, Sean O Faoláin and Peadar O'Donnell. It was called Common Ground and did for a while allow an exchange of views on subjects that interested the participants. The one burning subject for the writers was the operation of a Censorship Board which, though a state organ, was, for them, influenced by the church. In this they were right. Frank tried to assuage their irate feelings by telling those whom he particularly trusted that he had suffered much more from ecclesiastical authority than had they.

Leon was eventually given a top position in the Civil Service. He was appointed Secretary of Posts and Telegraphs. I had taught his children and grandchildren in Blackrock College and was now very close to the family. I enjoyed the confidence of his daughter Nóirín who gave up an important post to enter Carmel. I felt a kind of family pride in seeing the widening influence which her father had. A member of international or European commissions on Posts and Telecommunications or broadcasting, his contribution to such bodies would be on a high moral and cultural level. He was a splendid ambassador for our country, something that was seen in the kind of people from abroad who would love to spend time with him and his family.

There was every reason for *otium cum dignitate*. But when this brilliant man retired, it was to enter on a new career which brought him praise from the discerning. He had already works in Irish history to his credit, notably a substantial work on Parnell. He now became a prolific writer on recent Irish history. He had, while still in government service, done a documented study of the 1916 Rising seen from the British side. There now came a series of valuable monographs, the last of which, on Judge Miley, appeared not too long before the author's death.

Leon and I had many meetings, seasoned by something to eat and drink, with Frank Duff. When Frank died, such meetings still took place monthly, with a mutual friend, one of our ilk in many ways, completing the trio. This was Seamus Grace, a colleague on the teaching staff of Blackrock College, former Legionary envoy to Latin America, and like Leon and myself a member of the Dublin branch of the Ecumenical Society of the Blessed Virgin Mary. Our visits to Leon as he approached the narrows were poignant to a degree but truly uplifting. I was not with him as he died; I had been with him in St Vincent's Hospital within minutes of the death of his beloved wife, Cáit. She would deserve a whole chapter in this book, so noble and faithful was she.

How do I see Leon and Frank as time passes? Leon is easier to access. He had much in common with Frank, a sense of humour, a true love for Ireland, strong faith, notable success in the transfer of skills. He was equable in temperament, loved humorous stories especially about Dubliners, and to intimate friends he would narrate some of his episodes with politicians. Writing gave him fulfilment, and with his family he was immensely happy.

He loved and admired Frank. He would laud him for his fidelity, telling how he went every year with a group to the Cistercian Abbey in Mount Melleray, and to Lough Derg; he used to remind me how blessed we were to know this truly remarkable man. I think that, like myself, he considered Frank a saint. I think that comes through in his biography of his friend.

Was Frank a saint? Proponents of his cause will expand all that I have here sketched on his contribution to the church. Once on a guided tour of the Vatican he was shown the chair where the Pope sat when addressing meetings. If he were there and had one word to pronounce what would it be? 'Convert.' When I read this in the life of him which Hilda Firtel wrote, I remembered something he said to me: 'I would go to hell for a soul.' I think that it was on the same occasion that he said that when he would meet the Master and thought of what to say on his own behalf, he would not mention such things as his daily recitation of the Divine Office. No, he would say that on certain occasions he had risked being 'blotted out' for him, and had gone ahead. For of course Frank Duff was courageous to the marrow of his bones.

There were extraordinary graces in his life, but he had a cast-iron rule of silence on these things. I heard reliably that, about the time that he was completing the *Handbook*, he was, on the avenue in Mount Melleray, suddenly seized, raised into the air and thrown on the ground. In the sitting room of his house one evening he saw four pictures fall off the walls. Within two years four members of his family died.

As I check these pages before printing, I am due to participate in the opening ceremony in his Beatification process. Judge the tree by its fruits. The Legion exists in 160 countries, has an estimated active membership of three and three quarter million, with auxiliary members possibly ten times that number.

12. Scientists

I

Like many, perhaps most, priests I was educated without much contact with science, by which I mean the physical sciences. We did a little chemistry and physics in the first years before the programme became serious. My only memory of it is trying with wax and acid to get my name or my initials on a penny: subject to correction one covered the surface with molten candle wax, cut out the letters needed, poured on the acid and, hey presto, when all the wax was cleared away, you had letters shining bright.

I was reminded of such early academic trivia when one evening at a meeting of some society at University College, Dublin, a speaker who was a past pupil of our own St Mary's College, launched an attack on the Catholic secondary colleges for their neglect of the physical sciences. I was surprised and those who had invited me as a speaker were embarrassed. As often in such moments, one thinks of the reply later on. At the time three past pupils of my own college were professors in the faculties of science in our universities and a fourth was in the Higher Institute.

Yet for me as for many priests the physical sciences were a kind of vacuum. This is all the more strange if one considers the fact that for centuries priests were leaders in scientific research. I do not intend to enter into the question of science and faith, an area unnecessarily tangled, though signs of harmony are beginning to appear. I note in passing that in the summer of 1992 a remarkable contribution to this subject appeared in France. The veteran Catholic writer, Jean Guitton, nonagenarian, a philosopher, engaged in sustained dialogue with two eminent scientists, the brothers Bogdanov, teasing out many of the questions which crop up when the subject is mentioned. The book containing this dialogue was a runaway best seller at a rate of six thousand copies a day.

I shall write of two scientists whom I have known, one rather well, Alfred O'Rahilly, and the other a recent acquaintance, Rand McNally. Each reached a very high level of knowledge in his special field. But whereas Alfred diversified extensively, studying and writing on a variety of subjects, not satisfied to stay with Mathematical Physics of which he was Professor in University College, Cork, Rand McNally, to my knowledge, spoke and wrote on one subject, atomic science. On this he spoke with authority and what he said is relevant to the lives and possible deaths of us all. Like Alfred, he was a committed Catholic, fervent in practice.

I have no need to give the biography of Alfred O'Rahilly. That has been done in exemplary fashion by the priest historian, J. Anthony Gaughan; he has needed four volumes to exhaust the subject. I add some personal reminiscence. I was, with Fr Con Daly, joint editor of the Blackrock College Annual, revived in 1942 after three years in limbo as a result of the war. College Annuals like, and rightly I think, to feature past students. Alfred and his brother Thomas, the Irish historian, were ours. I had met him at a Legion of Mary function and perceived that he had some grievance against his Alma Mater. He thought too much attention was being given to Mr de Valera – with whom he had an on- off political relationship. I cannot refrain from quoting his quip, written in the *Catholic Standard* in answer to someone who had congratulated him on a book entitled *The Two Patricks* which was actually written by his brother: 'It's the two Devs that I'm interested in.' Whenever they met he and Dev got on famously; he must have been one of the few people who spoke to Dev with the abbreviation. Mrs de Valera certainly did.

We approached Alfred and he sent us an article which duly appeared in the College Annual. Before very long a distinguished past student, Dr John D'Alton, former president of Maynooth College, then ordinary of Meath diocese, now Archbishop of Armagh, was named a cardinal. We wished to honour him and we invited to the ceremony his contemporaries still living, among them Alfred. He stayed with us and on the eve of the gathering he consented to address the boys. He told them that Mr de Valera had been with him in the college as a boy. They had been on the special outing given to prize-winners, the Galaxy. Young de Valera was interested in translating the *Veni Creator Spiritus*. Alfred turned to me and threw off the remark: 'He's been translating a few other things since then.' He never lost the impish strain.

II

A few months later his wife died. We were represented at the funeral, which touched him. Soon afterwards I was called to the phone by Mrs Kevin O'Shiel (née Cecil Smiddy, a family closely united to Alfred in Cork, long-term friends). She told me that our mutual friend was staying with his sister Cecil, and was suffering delayed shock due to the decease of his wife. I told her to ask him to call on me. He did so and our conversation was surprising. I saw that he was still profoundly upset. But the surprise was his statement that he wished to become a priest. He had been with the Jesuits up to the first year in theology, when he left them. All through the subsequent years, of academic teaching and administration, political involvement, with imprisonment, projects of different kinds in the social domain, and incessant literary productivity, he had a dream, a hope that one day he would be a priest.

Next day I gave my superior, Fr Vincent Dinan, an account of my meeting with Alfred, especially of his expressed desire to be a priest. Fr Dinan reacted characteristically. 'Michael,' he exclaimed, 'it's like Newman.' The reference was to the scale, not the precise meaning of Alfred's desire. Fr Dinan remained true to his initial intuition, and saw our friend ordained priest in the college chapel, where as a boy he had seen the priestly ordination of Bishop Joseph Shanahan.

Things had not gone easily. Everything depended on the Archbishop of Dublin who at first had been cooperative, then seemed to change. We now know that discouraging messages had been sent to him and there were problems in church law as to the ecclesiastical authority which would sponsor the ordination. We were at a standstill. At the time Fr Dinan and I attended a funeral at Glasnevin and on the way home went to visit Alfred who was in the Bon Secours Hospital recovering from minor surgery. He was plainly depressed, more so as he had been reading a book of memoirs of an ex-Jesuit, which represented him – without giving his name – disparagingly.

After leaving him I pleaded with Fr Dinan, a close friend of Dr McQuaid. What harm could it do anyone to have Alfred ordained? Wasn't it really unbearable to see him so frustrated? My superior promised to intervene where it counted. As a result things were settled and the way was clear to the priesthood. There was no need to insist on studies. Alfred had been abreast of theological developments, and had a lively interest in biblical studies.

III

When Fr O'Rahilly had settled in to our community one could measure the scope of his learning. Fr Gaughan has given the complete bibliography of one who really deserved the title polymath; there were substantial works like his treatise on *Money*, occasioned by his membership of a commission on banking, a massive book on *Electromagnetics*, a monograph on the *Family at Bethany*, which with articles in the *Irish Ecclesiastical Record* signalled his interest in New Testament studies, a whole series of shorter books on such subjects as science and religion, social questions – I am tempted to add, etc. One must not forget his first full-length book, a life of the Irish Jesuit who died a chaplain in World War I, Fr Willie Doyle; this book was very widely translated; it was very thoroughly documented.

Alfred had been interested in the Shroud of Turin, on which he had made a valuable set of slides. Meanwhile he had amassed much documentation on the passion and death of Jesus. It took book form, as far as the page proof stage, in the hands of Fr James Bastible, Dean of Residence in University College, Cork, in the early fifties. Fr Bastible allowed me read it. The author did not publish it then and he put off requests from a Dublin publisher to issue it when he had come to live with us. Fr Gaughan published it after his death: *The Crucified*.

I think that it was as a result of his study of the passion of Jesus that his intellectual curiosity was aroused about Teresa Neumann, the Bavarian stigmatist (d. 1962). He clashed controversially with the German patristic scholar, resident in England, Hilda Graef, who wrote a book on Teresa in sceptical vein. He went to see the stigmatist and wrote a series of articles on her. Alfred was not overmuch given to controversy after his ordination, with the exception of the Trinity College debate which his friends, myself included, regretted; and a skirmish with another past student of ours, Myles na gCopaleen.

We expected that he would tackle a work which attracted him, on which he had collected vast materials and assembled books, a *Life of Christ*. But it is now increasingly felt, though not universally, that such a work is not the kind expected from biblical scholars. I say not universally, for though respected opinion seems against it, two excellent English scholars, Vincent Taylor and C. H. Dodd, did produce something like a life of Christ. Alfred did a popular work entitled *Gospel Meditations*. I think that, though his knowledge and his methodology were adequate, he was diffident about entering a field which he came to see as very demanding. There was too the question of age, and competing interests. He surprised us not too long before his death with the information that he was studying optics in the most advanced modern theories, and was even thinking of publishing something on the subject.

IV

What are my impressions of this unusual individual? I owe him an immense debt of gratitude for giving me access to his private library, letting me look over his vast treasury of handwritten notes, giving me his time, above all communicating something of his conviction that anything to do with religion should, when presented, conform to the most exacting demands of scholarship. His notes were classified in envelopes, on detachable slips of paper varying in size. His script was like print of a special kind; he told me that printers were as happy with it as with typescript.

Alfred's generosity was painful. You dare not mention a book you needed lest he offer at once to buy it for you. A friend in a spot of trouble visited us once. As he left Alfred turned to me: 'Will I write a cheque for a hundred pounds?' 'You'll do nothing of the kind,' I replied, 'he has rich relatives.' A hundred pounds was then a considerable amount of money.

I must admit that he was a bit inconsistent in his reactions to persons and projects. I understood this. I came to realise that he was a near genius and such people differ from the rest of us. Like many people of that kind he was not strong on self-knowledge. This is a gift that has apparently little to do with intellectual power, but I am not presenting a thesis on depth psychology. His failure to direct a scheme of adult education in Dublin similar to the successful one he had launched in Munster was a disappointment; his temperament may have complicated matters.

He had his temperament increasingly under control as the priesthood filled his life. His strong, simple faith was rocklike. Once I asked him what he thought of controversies about Adam and Eve; I knew that he had studied evolutionary theory. 'I make an act of faith,' he said quite simply. I have occasionally surprised people by telling them that his mode of expression varied as he spoke on subjects which he possessed completely and on matters which affected him emotionally but on which his information might be deficient. He was delightfully guarded when speaking on a subject he had mastered; he might be unduly assertive on others less well known to him.

A final word: there was greatness in him; he had dealt with great personalities, achievers, on a large scale, at home and abroad. Contact with such a person is inevitably formative. To have known Alfred (later Mgr) O'Rahilly was a blessing.

V

I have had less contact with Rand McNally. I came to know of him first when I was given a video made to dramatise certain moments in his career. It is called *A State of Emergency* and unfolds the scenario which would become reality in a particular situation. That situation is a nuclear tornado. The ultimate atomic bomb would not be a weapon to be used by any power to its advantage. It would ignite the atmosphere and circling the globe would reduce everything on its path to cinders. The issue is not one of military advantage, but of indiscriminate annihilation.

After viewing this video I had the idea of arranging a lecture by the author depicted in it. I thought that the Newman Society in University College, Dublin, members of which are friends, would invite Rand McNally to a meeting. I spoke to him of the possibility before putting the matter to them. His health seemed to rule out lengthy travel. I thus got to know him and have been honoured to receive from him copies of lectures he has given to learned scientific societies. These are unique publications, for they combine what to the lay mind looks like the most sophisticated exposition of scientific themes with frank evocation of specifically Catholic events of an extraordinary kind. I shall illustrate this presently. First, hear what he says of the 'megaton range fission-fusion bomb exploded by the US in the Pacific in 1958, at about forty-eight miles altitude'. The fireball expanded to about two hundred miles in diameter, was accompanied by a giant red shock-wave six hundred miles wide, photographed from Hawaii seven hundred and eighty miles away, with magnetic field perturbations observed twelve hundred miles away.

Rand McNally was not a reporter from outside on these awesome happenings. He had worked at atomic energy programmes for thirty years, was then a Fusion Energy Consultant, and had behind him a long series of scientific achievements and academic awards beginning with a brilliant course in Boston College, the Jesuit University.

The scientist was deeply concerned about the possibility of a nuclear tornado. The possibility had been studied by those qualified and their papers 'classified'. Rand prepared in 1973, when the documents were 'declassifed', a paper which he read at his own expense in that year at the International Atomic Energy Conference in Paris. Let me quote him on his further activity: 'The author also prepared in 1975 a slightly more detailed paper on fusion chain reactions referencing the declassified documents on this question of ignition of the atmosphere and alluded to the nuclear tornado hazard. Although this paper was rejected by *Science* magazine in June of 1975, a copy was sent in July to a Russian scientist known for his opposition to the gigantic Soviet tests of 1961.'

The title of another paper was *The Nuclear Dynamo – Can a nuclear tornado annihilate nations?* The author returned to the subject in an abstract presented to the thirty-third annual meeting of the Division of Plasma Physics. His title was *Is there a Doomsday Bomb?* He maintained that there was need for study of the essential question, and thought that this research 'might result in the complete banning of all so-called hydrogen or fusion bombs from the nations' arsenals'. Again he concluded that there should be 'an unclassified, international study of this question'. What a courageous stand!

VI

Rand McNally's special expertise distinguished him from Alfred O'Rahilly. But they met in a more important area, that in which the Holy Spirit acts directly. Just as Alfred brought all his scientific acumen and experience to bear on the Shroud of Turin and on the mystical phenomena in Teresa Neumann's life, so Rand McNally showed his readiness to investigate apparitions of Our Lady and to relate fearlessly their content to the rigorous findings, or the frightening possibilities, disclosed by his scientific research.

The great scientist showed the relevance to a possible nuclear catastrophe of 2 Peter 3:10: 'The day of the Lord will come as a thief; at that time the heavens will pass away with great violence, and the elements will be dissolved with heat, and the earth and the works that are in it will be burned up.'

Rand told me that he had gone twice to Fatima. I knew from a mutual friend that his first act every day was to say the rosary. We shall not be surprised then to read such words as these from him: 'Our Blessed Mother told Lucia (the Visionary of Fatima) ..."If people do not repent, Russia shall spread her errors throughout the world, promoting wars and persecution of the church; the good will be martyred, the Holy Father will have much to suffer, and various nations will be annihilated." ...To Sister Agnes Sasagawa in Akita, Our Lady said in part ..."If men do not repent and better themselves, the Father will inflict a terrible punishment on all humanity. It will be a punishment greater than the deluge ... Fire will fall from the sky and will wipe out a great part of humanity, the good as well as the bad, sparing neither priests nor faithful." To Julia of Naju in Korea Our Lady spoke also of "fire from heaven ... the chastisement could come through the human race itself; that is through a third world war and a nuclear war."'

The author of these words was the first scientist to set forth all the evidence needed to judge the giant aurora of January 25/26, 1938 and relate it to Our Lady's promise made at Fatima that there would be a great sign of this kind before the outbreak of the Second World War.

When the great atomic scientist accepted the invitation which I tendered to him on behalf of the organising committee of a Dublin congress on the 'Alliance of the two Hearts' to come as a speaker, I had two moments of anxiety: As he was advancing in years would his voice carry in the large hall? Because of his very expertise would the audience understand him? He was in each respect a complete success.

With such evidence, brief as it has to be, the reader may not find a comparison of Rand McNally with Louis Pasteur far-fetched.

Did I meet any other scientist of similar outlook and quality? Yes, but so briefly that I can but name him, Dr Karl Philberth. He and his brother Bernhard are nuclear physicists. They are also prestigious inventors, with one hundred patents to their credit. They are consulted by highly placed authorities in church and state, not excluding military commanders. They were both ordained priests in 1972. If all their published work is of the same quality as the one essay which Fr Karl gave me, a paper read to the International Congress of the World Federation of Doctors who respect human life, he would be in the company of Alfred O'Rahilly and Rand McNally. I think that we shall see more scientists like all three. I cherish the hope that we shall enter soon an era when theologians and scientists are not mutually distrustful, even in opposition to each other, but conscious of mutual assistance, enlightenment and support.

This hope was strengthened in me as I listened to Rand McNally at the congress on the 'Alliance of the Two Hearts' held in Dublin, 23-25 September 1994.

13. The Philippines and Medjugorje

I

I have visited this blessed land four times. I do not, in setting down some memories, claim to convey the magic of the people, their distinctive characteristics, nor the inner religious fibre which makes them the hope of the Catholic Church in the continent of Asia. I write to record privileged experience. I should perhaps first relate a strange story which came to light about the Philippines after World War Two. During the war the authorities of the Legion of Mary in Dublin received from time to time accounts of the fortunes of their members, numerous in the country. Towards the end of the hostilities the name of a Japanese general came up, one strangely sympathetic to Catholics. People in Dublin were mystified: Who was he? Was he reliable?

The mystery was solved at a public meeting in Dublin which I attended. The Archbishop of Manila, Dr Michael O'Doherty, was present at a meeting of Concilium Legionis, the governing body of the Legion of Mary. Dr O'Doherty had lived through the war and knew the Japanese occupation at first hand. One day a Japanese general was announced. Such a visitor until then meant trouble, demands of a kind that would cause hurt to the church, and to those representing it in the different sectors of the people's life. With a sense of foreboding he asked that the general be brought to his office. He went to the door to receive him and was surprised to see him kneel and kiss his episcopal ring respectfully.

'Are you of the household of the faith' Dr O'Doherty enquired of his visitor. 'Yes, your Grace, I am a Catholic and I am half Irish; my mother was born in county Cork.' Then the archbishop heard an unusual story. An official at the London Japanese embassy had met an Irish girl, whom he wished to marry. She agreed, provided he accept the Church's conditions. He did so and this was their son. The father insisted on the baptismal name Francis Xavier, best known Catholic saint in the Far East. 'But,' said the archbishop's visitor, 'my mother got her say in my confirmation, adding Patrick.' So he was Patrick Francis Xavier Walsh Sassu. He had come to tell Dr O'Doherty that he had been appointed to take charge of religious affairs in the Philippines. He would do all in his power to help Catholics, but he must be circumspect. He was true to his word. Sadly, when the war ended, he disappeared. The worst was suspected.

I tell elsewhere the story of the symposium on the *Alliance of the two Hearts* organised by the Filippinos in Fatima in 1986. This ideal has been taken up across the Catholic world. I have stated in public that this powerful intuition coming from the Holy Father is the gift of Philippine Catholics to the whole church. I heard John Paul II say just that in the course of an audience.

In the year following the symposium I was invited to participate in the congress in Manila which would aim at extending the message of the Two Hearts to the faithful. The Cardinals Sin and Vidal, who gave the congress their patronage, and those who did the planning and organising, Fr Catalino Arevalo, SJ, of the Manila Ateneo and Ambassador Howard Dee, inspired great confidence; their work was rewarded by a splendid meeting in Manila Convention Centre. Fr René Laurentin, like myself a symposium member, was present as was the Rector of Fatima Sanctuary, Mgr Luciano Guerra.

II

Travelling to lecture in other centres I met wonderful people. I mention Fr Niall O'Brien first because he is a past pupil of mine, and he figured in a bizarre case of persecution during the last months of the Marcos regime. He is a Columban father, within a great tradition of missionary work in the Philippines, as elsewhere. Niall was put in jail on the pretext that he had been involved in the murder of the mayor of his town. The charge was not only unjust, but preposterous, as anyone who knows him will testify. There was another bizarre turn of events. One day Fintan Drury of RTÉ, a friend, called me on the phone and told me not to miss an item on that day's programme. It was a live interview with Fr Niall direct from his prison cell. There too he was able to answer telephone calls, and as far as I remember, one of those who called him was Cardinal Ó Fiaich, Primate of all Ireland.

I spent an evening with him now in happier times, delighted to find not a trace of his grim experience in his bearing, conversation or reflexes. He was editing a missionary magazine which, to judge by the issue I saw, was bright, topical and modern in presentation and news. He was also deeply involved with the non-violence movement, and had just completed a book on the spirituality of non-violence.

I think that it may have been Niall who introduced me to Bishop Forteich, his bishop, who had stood by him during his mock trial. Bishop Forteich was the voice of social justice in the Philippines. He was disliked by a section of the privileged class. He was disliked still more by the officials of the Marcos regime. He told me that while he was in Singapore some time previously to receive the Magsasay award – a Far Eastern version of the Nobel Peace Prize – his episcopal residence had been burned down. What was the purpose of this incendiary attack? Destruction of revealing archives stored in a part of the house. The archives related the crimes of the military in the days of Marcos. Again I refer to Fintan Drury, who informed me that he had seen the store of incriminating documents, and photographed it for his programme on the Philippines.

Bishop Forteich told me of an attack on his temporary residence. A hand grenade was thrown into an open space in front of the house, possibly meant for him personally. It didn't seem to worry him unduly. The incident occurred during the night, and when he told the investigating police that he was going back to bed they were quite surprised. Nothing else happened.

During that same visit to the country I spent a night in the apartment adjoining the Carmelite convent in Cebu. After Mass next morning I met the sisters. They told me that it was they who hid President Corazon ('Cory') Aquino the night before she was flown back to claim the presidency to which she had been elected despite attempts at rigging the ballot. I asked if she had used the apartment where I stayed. Not at all, the Mother Prioress told me. She was kept in a cell within the enclosure. All night there was banging on the door, which they took for attempts from a death squad to gain entrance. It was her own sympathisers looking for her. Next morning when the sisters were reassured, they released their precious lodger.

III

I think that it is regrettable that the story of the Philippine crisis which ended the Marcos regime, and the manner in which it was resolved, is not more widely known. I think that it is especially regrettable that the Yugoslav hierarchy had not reflected on this amazing chain of events. I recall some of the events which I have heard from reliable witnesses, and which are documented with total accuracy in the book of the peaceful revolution, which is entitled *People Power: An Eyewitness History*, a collection of testimonies published in the critical year, when all was over, 1986.

Marcos had been declared president by the National Assembly, but the Minister of Defence, Juan Ponce Enrile, and the Deputy Chief of Staff, Fidel Ramos, knew that Cory Aquino had been truly elected. They knew that the Catholic bishops agreed with them. When they raised the standard of revolt they had few followers. Ramos then called Cardinal Sin on the telephone. Let the Cardinal tell the story: 'On Saturday afternoon, as I was about to go the Ateneo for the ordination of two Jesuits, Cristina Ponce Enrile called me, crying: "Cardinal, help us." Then Juan Ponce Enrile called: "Cardinal, I will be dead in one hour." And he seemed to be trembling: "I don't want to die,' he added. "But if it is possible, do something. I'd still like to live. I already heard the order to smash us." He was almost crying.

Then Fidel Ramos, who is a Methodist, told me that he embraced the image of Our Lady of Fatima. "Dear Lady," he had said, "I know that you are miraculous." And he told me: "Cardinal, help us by calling the people to support us."'

Cardinal Sin promised his help, saying that the place would be full of people. He first telephoned the Prioress of each of the convents of contemplative sisters and urged them to begin a period of intense prayer. Then he called Radio Veritas, the free station operated by June Keithley, and through this medium called on the people to go out and rally to the support of the insurgents. Soon three million people were in the streets between the two armies. The history of this unparalleled exercise in democracy needs far more scope than I can give it.

I write of the event because the Philippines which I have come to know and love has been fashioned by it, and because I have had personal memories related to me by survivors of a heroic moment in world history. I have come to know very well June Keithley Castro who, in face of terrible odds and constant adverse pressure, kept Radio Veritas on the air and provided a vital link between those challenging Marcos and the people. She is still active in Catholic communications and has, among other important services, brought the full light of truth to bear on the apparition of Our Lady over forty years ago in Lipa, about which I have written.

With Fr René Laurentin I interviewed a Manila lady whose husband is at the head of a large business. She held up her rosary and said to us: 'As I left the house each morning, I showed this to my family and said, "If I do not come back, I shall have died for this and the Philippines".' To Fr Laurentin and myself Cardinal Sin related a singular tale. The crisis was over in effect when four of the five helicopter gunships, sent out to crush or disperse the assembled people, changed sides and went over to the insurgents. It is commonly said that this decision was taken after the commanding officer looked down and saw the people form a cross beneath his gaze.

The Cardinal's narrative turned on something equally potent, but dissimilar. After the crisis, a group of young soldiers came to his residence and told him something they thought he should know. At a critical moment, when tension was mounting in the streets, they were ordered to fire on the massed civilians who had no weapons but their statues of Our Lady of Fatima and their rosary beads. But suddenly a globe of light appeared before them and a woman gleaming with power stepped out. 'I am the Queen of this country,' she said, 'do not shoot my children.' They obeyed her, not their officer.

EDSA is the name of the spot in Manila where people power was so effective (the initials are of *Epiphania de los Santos*). Today a splendid statue of Our Lady commemorates the mighty event.

President Aquino, in her letter of thanks to Cardinal Sin, rightly expressed her gratitude not only for people power, but 'prayer power'. I asked Howard Dee once if it was true that Our Lady had said, long before the event, that the first manifestation of her Immaculate Heart would be in the Philippines. He assured me that he had stated this in public lectures. It has been wonderful to visit a land so favoured.

But the Filippino bishops had shown their faith in the Mother of God. They had declared a Marian Year to commemorate Our Lady's birth, followed by a Eucharistic Year to commemorate the fiftieth anniversary of the first International Eucharistic Congress held in Asia, in Manila in 1937. This culminated in the congress on the Alliance of the Two Hearts, which I have mentioned. They had in EDSA the reward of their faith.

IV

Would the Yugoslav bishops have had a similar reward if they had made an act of faith in Our Lady of Medjugorje? I personally think so. When they met to consider the findings of the commission which they had established, they had evidence of a kind never before seen, even possible, in the evaluation of a supernatural event. They had overwhelming proof of the *sensus fidelium,* the reliable sentiment of the faithful. What are the particulars? In sixteen years over twenty-two million pilgrims have gone to

Medjugorje, more than twenty thousand priests, one hundred bishops. They go to pray and in many cases to return to God from a life of indifference towards him. One hundred and fifty priests were at times needed for confessions – something unique in the whole world in recent times.

Beyond Medjugorje itself is the worldwide global fraternity stirred to a new life by its message. How many prayer groups have arisen throughout the church as a direct result of Medjugorje? Five hundred have been mentioned for Austria. It is known that in three Australian cities, Melbourne, Brisbane and Sydney, there are six thousand. There may be tens of thousands in North and South America.

Scientific study of the witnesses has been of a kind not possible in the case of well-known apparitions which have been approved – La Salette, Rue du Bac, Lourdes, Fatima. All the resources of modern psychology and psychiatry have been used to help reach a judgement on the trustworthiness of the visionaries. The contents of their messages have been evaluated by theologians of indisputable competence. Theories put forward to explain the phenomena, such as hallucination, peasant psychology, manipulation, have been proved unsatisfactory.

Despite this totally favourable result of impartial inquiry, the Yugoslav bishops were found wanting. Did they act on the criterion given them by their Master, 'judge the tree by its fruits'? How could any but a supernatural cause produce such strictly supernatural effects: prayer, sacramental life, penance, conversion – in some cases after years of religious indifference and at every cultural level – miracles of healing and of reconciliation?

All this has come from God and the bishops, in their much-quoted statement of 27/28 November 1991, still had the tragic disbelief or cowardice to assert that they could not affirm that the origin of the apparitions or revelations was supernatural.

What do the Yugoslav bishops think is supernatural? Is the Catholic Church, which they represent, supernatural? How do they know? How does God manifest his supernatural power through its life?

It is well-known that the meeting of bishops where the statement was drawn up was stormy, the storm caused mostly by the Bishop of Mostar. It was said afterwards that the hierarchy did not wish to humiliate the Bishop of Mostar. Hence the question: is he more important than the Mother of God? After my first visit to Medjugorje I wrote to him to express my testimony. He sent me the memorandum which he had drawn up on the whole subject. In the two books which I wrote on Medjugorje I wished to be scrupulously fair to him; I published his text in full. The reader will see that it opens with his admission that when he first heard of the apparitions he thought that this would be the solution of his problem with the Franciscans: a question of their tenure of parochial administration where he did not want them.

V

Now, without passing any judgement on the bishop's conscience, can any Christian believer seriously think that the act of divine omnipotence needed for an apparition, would be forthcoming just to settle a dispute about parochial administration? Surely the primary purpose of the Lord and his Blessed Mother in such happenings is the conversion of sinners, the extension of the kingdom of God through his church, the glory of the Most Holy Trinity.

One member of the hierarchy saved the honour of the church. Archbishop Frane Franic of Split, already known at Vatican II, is the outstanding theologian of the Croatian hierarchy. He has been president of the episcopal theological commission, and was asked to continue in this office after his retirement on reaching the age limit. He has fully expressed his belief in the apparitions at Medjugorje. When last I met him I said, 'You have professed your belief in Our Lady of Medjugorje; she rewarded you by preserving the city of Split during the war.' His reply: 'I cannot deny that Split has been preserved.' The reader will know that Dubrovnik, not far away, was heavily damaged.

14. Two Cardinals

I

Since my youth I have had a certain idea about Poland, an idea touched with fixed emotion which deepened with the years. The Catholic faith had much to do with this. Here was a Catholic people with whom we had kinship, whom we could understand. This sentiment was nourished by my study of history and by one of my favourite authors, Hilaire Belloc. How well he summarised so much that he had written on Poland when in *Back to the Baltic* he spoke of a 'sacred flame' burning in this land.

I had, to my delight, Polish fellow students at the University of Fribourg. Since I am to set down here some memories of a great Polish Cardinal, I should recall something of the Polish agony that was World War II.

This agony was in two phases. The German forces invaded Polish soil on 1 September 1939, while the Russians moved in to take the agreed share of the national territory. The Poles, who had guarantees from the western powers, found themselves alone before the overwhelming German armour. The bravery of the Polish army was total, as was that of the Polish people during the years of military occupation. To enter into detail here would seem to foster animosity, which is far from my intention. The sufferings of this nation send us straight to the mystery of evil. Why did so many innocent people have to see their homes wrecked, their family life shattered, their future and that of their children blackened? Why did this people, who bore witness to God in so many ways denied him by others, suddenly appear helpless before massive wickedness? The most terrible death camps were established on Polish soil; citizens were tortured more than elsewhere; the capital city was, after the withdrawal of German forces, a scene of desolation unparalleled, eighty-five per cent of its buildings destroyed, a city of human emptiness.

This collective agony is briefly, serenely, recalled in one of the great Christian documents of this century, the letter sent by the Polish hierarchy to the bishops of Germany in 1966 to invite them to the ceremonies which, in that year, would mark the Polish Christian Millennium. It contains one stark statistic: Poland had lost six million citizens at the war's end.

All that is phase one of the Polish tragedy. The second began with the withdrawal of the German military and administrative forces. The power vacuum would be filled by Stalinists. The sombre keynote was struck when the Warsaw underground units rose in revolt against the Germans. The Poles counted on reinforcement from the Russian army already marching on the city. This help was denied them. Stalin halted his units some distance from the city to ensure the elimination of the heroic Polish fighters. He knew that they would not support his iniquitous masterplan; they would not consent to the subjugation of their nation.

With Polish communists, the Russian dictator effected the political take-over. The way had been cleared for him at Yalta, when the western powers sold out to one tyrant the splendid nation which they had allegedly fought to liberate from another. Not only was this inherent treachery. The monstrous act of cynicism added to the mental agony of the Poles. It opened a long stretch of oppression, omnipresent, callous, deeply offensive to a highly sensitive people.

The Poles suffered too from perverse economics. Marx had said that religion is the opium of the people. Marxism was the opium of the intellectuals, western economists who lauded a system about which they really knew nothing. They were at a safe distance from the reality. Those held in bondage by the Russians, not only in Poland but in all eastern Europe, paid with their personal security, livelihood and family happiness for the monstrous errors which, without dissent from many western economists, had been elevated into sacred dogma. All the world knows since the collapse of the marxist system in Russia and the dependencies, how right Solshenitsyn was when he wrote in his open letter to the rulers of his country, 'Do not forget that marxism has been the economic ruin of our country.'

My first acquaintance with this world was in the Millennium Year, 1966. Previously my Superior General, an Irishman, Fr Francis Griffin, had refused me permission to travel there; he was, as a result I think of a personal visit, conscious of danger for foreign priests. His successor, Mgr Marcel Lefebvre, gave me a favourable answer.

Complications arose immediately. My request to the Polish Embassy in London for a visa was not even acknowledged – there was no embassy or consulate in Dublin. A second request made by a travel agency on my behalf met with a blank refusal. Then I had an idea. I would seek a Russian visa and hope for a Polish transit visa on the way there and back. This would give me seventy-two hours going and coming. I telephoned the Russian Embassy in London and asked the official if they would give me a visa to enter his country. Certainly, he replied. He may have been influenced by the fact that my Dublin agency had, in a formal document, appointed me their representative. Peter Kilroy, my editor in the *Catholic Standard*, had also drawn up a statement giving me status. How long would it take to issue the visa? One day. 'This is Monday and I have to leave on Friday,' I said. 'How will you get your passport to us and back in that time?' 'I shall send it, and my agent's representative in London will collect passport and visa and deliver them to me on the way through London airport.' All of which happened.

I decided to stop in Brussels and visit the shrine of the Infant of Prague in that city. I had learned of his power from my mother. In Brussels, through the courtesy of an airport official, I was given hospitality in the great Jesuit College, St Michel – I have got to know it very well since then for other reasons. The Polish consulate was nearby. I went there and, as I entered, met a woman who seemed sympathetic. I said to her somewhat emotionally: 'How is it that I can go to any country in the east except yours, the only one I really want to visit?' She urged me to slow down and make my request. The Vice-consul gave me a form and asked me to fill it up, adding a photograph; fortunately I had one. He would put the matter before the Consul, due back shortly. Coming out of the sanctuary of the Infant of Prague I telephoned the consulate. Shall I ever forget his words, '*Votre visa est accordé*'? When could I collect it? Right now. I hopped into a taxi and in no time had the magic document in my hands. That year many applications for visas were refused.

I arrived in Warsaw, and walked through its streets as if I was walking through a miracle. In fact I was. At the initial meeting of the provisional government after the war, the first proposal on the agenda was to abandon Warsaw because of its condition and establish a new capital in Lublin – this would be nearer Russia. One man objected, Hilary Minc. They should not leave Warsaw. They should rebuild it as it had been. The man's name will surely live forever. What he proposed has been done. Even the medieval market town, Stare Maestu, is still recognisable as it had been. The Poles don't get much credit for this astonishing achievement.

II

I had the great honour of meeting the Cardinal. His secretary didn't think he had the time. I asked him to show His Eminence a letter of thanks he had sent me for a financial gift I had sent him. I had been only an intermediary; the real donor was Máirín Ó Dálaigh, wife of the president. The secretary returned to lead me at once to the great man's presence.

I offered my sympathy for the ordeal he was enduring. This I must explain. Ten years previously, in 1956, in the crisis coinciding with the Hungarian rising, Gomulka, newly installed, had released the Cardinal from detention. They needed him to maintain political stability. His prestige was enormous as had been seen on the preceding 26 August, feast of Our Lady of Czestochowa. On that day over a million people had assembled at the shrine, using every makeshift form of transport or none.

High above the vast multitude was an empty chair decked in red and white, the national colours. Everyone knew who should be there – Wyzshinski, still imprisoned. He was released to universal relief. His presence in Warsaw was powerfully beneficial. He supported political order and everyone knew that he was utterly incorruptible. He used a telling phrase: 'Poles have shown they can die for their country, now they must show they can live for Poland.'

Now we are in 1966, which was widely considered the Church's Millennium. The political rulers thought that the time had come to eliminate the Cardinal. A ferocious attack was launched on him through all government-controlled media. The pretext was the letter he and the other bishops had sent to the German bishops. He was depicted as a traitor, dealing with the enemy. That it was a pretext and a silly one was evident some years later when the government made a deal with Germany.

The Cardinal's patriotism was defended by the hierarchy led by the Archbishop of Cracow, Karol Wojtyla. The people I met told me they were sick to death of being bludgeoned by the media. It merely served to enhance the Cardinal's figure as a national hero. When I met him and spoke with him, he showed signs of stress, but his morale was awe-inspiring. I told him that I had followed the attempts to misrepresent him and those who were defending him. An article in the great Jesuit review, *La Civiltá Catolica,* had been truncated to pervert the writer's sense. He was aware of this.

On the question of the regime he assured me that he did not interfere in politics. He was the leader of a homogeneously Catholic people who had learned, instinctively, a valuable lesson: 'You can't put the whole town in jail.' If they all practised their religion the agents of the regime could do nothing about it. I told him that I was going on to Russia for a few days, and he advised me to be careful. How did I feel? Rather like a tyro taking a first dip being told by a Channel swimmer to look out! It was a caring gesture. We talked about the Pope, Paul VI, who as a young Curia official had spent a short time in Poland at the nunciature. The Cardinal asked me if I should see him to assure him that they were hoping he would come for the Millennium celebration.

On the plane to Moscow I met three Americans, Charles Percy and two aides. Charles Percy was a senatorial candidate in the forthcoming elections, and he was doing the ethnic tour, going on to Lithuania and Hungary – there was a Polish, Lithuanian and Hungarian vote in his state, Illinois. He had been disappointed not to have met Wyzshinski. On the way from the airport to the city I was a guest in the limousine sent for him; he recorded my impressions. He would be in the Gelert Hotel in Budapest on Easter Sunday. I was to remember this.

Moscow was fascinating, but I shall stay with Poland. Back in Warsaw I was able to attend at the Holy Thursday ceremony presided over by the Cardinal. The congregation was diverse, but when he stood in the pulpit, all followed him with rapt attention. One sentence he spoke was memorable. Pointing to the old men at the end of the church whose feet he would wash in the Mandatum ceremony, he said: 'To night I would wash the feet of anyone in the world, even of those who consider me their enemy.' The presence in the congregation of one individual, obviously Indian, intrigued me. What was he doing here?

The Cardinal was to preach again on Easter Sunday. I mentioned this to a Polish priest with whom I had lunch in a crowded restaurant, adding that I was sorry I could not be at this Mass. 'Oh,' said my friend, without lowering his voice, 'you can always get the text from the Secret Police.' The Polish Canadian priest who was with us was as apprehensive as I was for our friend. He himself did not worry in the slightest. Leon O'Broin told me of a similar experience he had at that time. He was a member of a government delegation and the waiter in their restaurant was telling them out loud what he thought of things. 'Go easy,' someone said to him, 'they'll put you in jail.' 'So what,' was the reply, 'we've all been in jail.' There was something of that in Wyzshinski!

I later read the text of the Cardinal's Easter homily. He recalled the darkest moment of the war, the year 1944. As he made his way through the city on Easter Sunday night, a stranger accosted him and cried out: 'Priest of God, Christ is risen and Poland will rise.' The Cardinal was expressing this enduring hope in 1966. I must admit that another thought crossed my mind. He was subtly reminding those now persecuting him that he was in Warsaw in its hour of deepest agony; some of them were, at the time, in safe keeping with their Russian patrons in Moscow.

III

I left Warsaw in a mood of exhilaration with memories which are still fresh. I was on my way to Budapest where, I had been assured by my travel agent, I would easily obtain a transit visa. A surprise awaited me.

The woman who gave me the required form took my passport and directed me to the transit lounge. 'How long will it take?' 'About half an hour.' Nothing happened after half an hour, nor after an hour. The women at the desk looked embarrassed; one of them offered me some of her luncheon, as I was not allowed to leave the transit lounge, where I was now alone. These women were gentle and respectful, with one exception, the one who seemed senior, who was hard faced. I asked her how long more it would take. 'Perhaps two hours, if you get it.' I was suddenly conscious of isolation. I thought of what I had written in the *Leader* on the Hungarian rising and its repression. The title of my piece, *Holocaust*, would not win me friends among the secret police, one of whom was now wrestling with my request for a visa. The fact that it was Easter Sunday, I was informed later, meant that only one was on duty. Hence the delay, for in that world no one wanted to be the sole signatory of an important document.

To break the monotony and the sense of isolation I decided to call Mr Percy. I told him of my predicament and that I would not now get my train to Györ in western Hungary. He was very warm-hearted and if I must spend the night in the city he would speak on my behalf to the manager of the Gelert Hotel. For fiscal reasons it would scarcely be my choice.

Four hours passed before they let me go. With my passport and their visa I went out into the departure hall. Here I behaved rather imprudently. I complained to the woman who had first taken my request. Did they detain me because I was honest, showing on my passport that I was a priest? She made a gesture which I shall not forget. She described a circle with her right hand, then made a small space with her thumb and forefinger. 'I'm only this in that.'

I went to the currency desk and met a kind, motherly woman. 'They kept me four hours in there,' I said 'and now I've missed my train.' 'Yes,' she replied, 'I heard about it. Easy! you've got your visa. I'll get you a taxi and a hotel.' So I was soon at the 'Liberty' Hotel. Here everyone was courteous. In the restaurant the customary violinist was answering a request from a large group in the far corner, Americans teaching in Europe I learned later. What had they requested? 'It's a long way to Tipperary!'

IV

Next day I was at Györ, saying Mass at the shrine of the Irish Madonna. It had been brought to the city by Walter Lynch, the exiled Bishop of Clonfert, in Cromwellian times. He was accepted as assistant bishop of Györ, and was buried in the cathedral. His picture, Italian in style, was enshrined in a special chapel. Among those who came to honour Our Lady here was Cardinal Mindszenty, who celebrated Mass and preached in the cathedral on 17 March 1947, the two hundred and fiftieth anniversary of a miracle.

The miracle took place on 17 March 1697, the darkest year in the oppression of Irish Catholics. On that day the image wept for several hours. The Calvinist minister, the town commandant and the Jewish Rabbi are mentioned as witnesses. I was shown cloths used to dry the tears. At the principal Mass, on this Easter Monday, I was delighted to hear a full choir render magnificently

Handel's Alleluiah chorus. Catholics in a communist-dominated country were not in the catacombs. I talked about the recent accord between the Vatican and the regime, which marked the first steps in *Ost-politik.*, with one of the priests. He simply shrugged his shoulders.

Next day, back in Budapest, I went to the American Embassy on 'Liberty' square. Cardinal Mindszenty was in residence there; he had just been able to enter the building before the short-lived 1956 rising was crushed; the insurgents had given him his freedom and we know from his memoirs what torture he had endured. There was no question for me of meeting him; any such encounter would need previous agreement by the governments of the US and Hungary. A visiting American with an eye to some advantage back home would occasionally claim the right to a meeting with the prisoner. The official who received me told me that they would lead him to the telephone, ask him to call the White House and obtain the authorisation. Otherwise they refused the request outright. It was their duty to protect the Cardinal and strict observance of protocol was imposed on them by their sense of duty.

With that statement of principle the embassy official proved otherwise very helpful and informative. They assumed that all the buildings at the rear of the Legation were in government control. These overlooked the small patio where the prisoner went every evening to take some exercise. But never alone. This they would not risk, so he always had a companion from the embassy staff. They could not of course prevent photography, which they thought was constantly exercised on the Cardinal.

How did he impress the official who was my informant? Profoundly, as I could see. He had learned English, so that the Catholics could assist at his Mass. He was rock-like in his powers of endurance. It is well known that he would have been 'pardoned' and released by the government if he had consented to ask forgiveness for the 'crimes' for which he had been unjustly condemned. He refused to do anything of the kind; his sense of honour absolutely forbade it. Thank God.

I left the Legation and, half way across the square, I was accosted by a hoodlum who spoke a few words in English about America, as far as I could follow him. When I looked back I saw him in earnest conversation with the military guards in front of the Legation. I assumed that everyone entering and leaving the Legation was photographed, at least observed, from the opposite side of the square. Was this fellow sent to test me?

Very shortly I was to see something rather different from this hard face of marxism. I stopped a gentleman who had just parked his car, to ask for information on how to get a bus to my hotel. He waved me to the car, invited me to sit in, and drove me there. The evening before I had returned from Györ by train, and had had a very interesting conversation with a lawyer and his wife and daughter. He had been a prisoner of war – 'war is war,' he said sadly. Though an atheist, he spoke very respectfully of Ireland: 'It is a very Catholic country.' His daughter would like to learn English. 'Here we're forced to learn Russian,' she explained disapprovingly. We left the train, he put me on the right bus and insisted on paying my fare.

IV

I was relieved to take the train to Austria, having been fortunate enough to find at the frontier some form or other which the last official on my journey needed. Then within a few minutes it was the warm greetings of Austrian frontier guards, with their Tyrolese hats and cherubic faces. What a different world. I stayed long enough in Vienna to visit the national Marian shrine at Mariazell, a spot loaded with eloquent history. Each morning I said Mass at the nearby *Schottenstiff,* welcomed with warm hospitality by the monks, conscious of the Irish origins of their monastery.

I went on to Rome and had the privilege of an audience with Paul VI. I fulfilled my promise to Cardinal Wyzshinski and told the Pope that the Poles were hoping he would visit them for the Millennium ceremonies. The Pope replied very simply: 'The government will not give me a visa.' When I told him I had gone to the American Legation in Budapest, he asked me very simply, pointing to my Roman collar: 'Dressed like that?' I reassured him.

A young Curia official called Casaroli also saw me. How could I know that this was a future Secretary of State? A French colleague of his in the Curia whom I met – he was leaving to become secretary to the French national episcopal conference – told me that he had a future; they thought he was in the mould of Pius XII.

Mgr Casaroli told me that they in Rome could not accept the Hungarian Primate's thesis that when the throne was vacant, he was the Regent. The young prelate was at the beginning of his *ost-politik* career. He admitted that it involved risk. But the Pope thought they had to try in some way to help the Catholics of eastern Europe. I do not intend to enter the debate on the *ost-politik* question. I have been reliably informed that Cardinal Wyzshinski thought it misguided. Defenders of the policy sometimes write as if it caused the changes in Russia and eastern Europe, which is not true. This was done by 'people power', the headline for which was set by the Filippinos in the streets of Manila during the 'Edsa' days of February 1986.

Two years later I was to visit again the three cities of Warsaw, Moscow and Budapest. I attended the meeting of the International Catholic Press Union in Berlin. The West Berlin authorities were very hospitable. They lost nothing as a consequence of this, as there were Catholic journalists from many countries present. At one of the general meetings I proposed that we send a telegram to the Polish Cardinal, a former journalist. Nothing came of it but a distinguished Indian came up to thank me, and we exchanged opinions about his Eminence. I said that I had seen him in a moment of power, on Holy Thursday evening, 1966; he was also there, he told me.

The whole conference was enlightening. The ideas of Vatican II were simmering here and there, sometimes on the boil which damaged them. A tendentious question being asked or implied was: 'Do we need a Catholic Press, now that the church is open to the modern world, as the title of a conciliar text declared?' I maintained, in conversation with an American priest of the Maryknoll Missionary Society, working on the Vatican news service, *Fides*, that it was a big risk to eliminate the Catholic press. The day might come when the secular press would turn hostile to the church. What then? He asked me to put this opinion to the assembly. I believe today more than ever in its validity. There is need today for a robust, professionally impeccable, unashamedly Catholic paper in every important meeting-place of ideas and human forces. The Catholic voice should be heard where people congregate to generate important future developments. In the word 'Catholic' I include what is truly ecumenical. The Catholic press should not lapse through the mistaken policy that caused the ending of some Catholic publishing houses.

V

With such ideas in my head and some happy memories of West Berlin, I went with a group of Catholic journalists to Warsaw. I could not pay my respects to the Cardinal as he was not in town. But I had a surprise. As I walked down the main street in the city I suddenly realised that the two Indians whom I had seen, one in Warsaw, the other in Berlin, were one and the same person. He was Peter Raina, a graduate of universities in Geneva and Oxford, author of the definitive, fully documented life of Cardinal Wyzshinski, written in Polish. The first volume appeared during the pre-liberation days, published in Berlin.

In Warsaw we met, on separate occasions, representatives of the three associations of Catholic writers, the Pax group who had links with the regime, the Catholic Social Association, more independent, the Znak people, totally so. At the meeting I was the only priest present who was in clerical attire. A photographer was very eager to get a picture of a priest meeting them. He kept moving about the room, only to find that I was able to shield myself with a newspaper, foiling his effort. I had been caught previously and saw my picture on the cover page of a Pax publication. This caused annoyance to one Polish bishop. He did not understand that when I was photographed before some statue or other I did not know the identity or allegiance of the cameraman.

From the Znak members we learned what it meant to be an independent, Catholic writer inside a marxist society. One told about the problem of getting a passport. One year you might get it, the next meet refusal, with no reason given: no redress. What courage these people had. I left the room where we met them with a feeling of awe.

We went on to Moscow, which I knew slightly from my previous visit. We were received in the office of *Isvestia* by representatives of the Russian press and review publications. The principal spokesman was the president of the union of Soviet journalists. He attacked American policy in South Vietnam. An American, who had condemned the American intervention in South Vietnam, put to him an embarrassing question. The questioner said: 'I have expressed these very views in my paper. What will be the reaction in your country if you condemn official government policy?' It was a bit unfair, some of us thought, for, within the narrow limits of their freedom, they were being generous to receive us at all. The reply was suitably fudged through the interpreter. I asked about the reaction in their reviews to John XXIII's Encyclical *Pacem in Terris*. I got a pleasant answer. There was some humourous banter.

VI

I have often related an incident which took place after the routine visit to Lenin's tomb, which was arranged for us with a minimum of time waiting; the queue stretched along Red Square. When we came out of the rigorously controlled sanctum – I saw a soldier pull away the hand of a man preceding me as it was in his trench-coat pocket. I asked our guide if this was a religious act. She stamped her little foot on the ground as she replied vehemently: 'No, it's nothing of the kind.' I was not surprised; I understood quite well that she did not wish us to spread the word through our papers that they were worshipping a corpse.

Then recalling the rich Russian tradition of piety towards Our Lady, whom they sometimes call the *Pokrov,* the Protectress, I asked her: 'Lara, do you love the Blessed Virgin Mary?' This time there was no protest. She just said rather meekly: 'Why should I?' All I could think of saying was: 'Because, spiritually speaking, she is the most beautiful woman in the world.' Lara just hung her little head a little.

That night, as we were assembled for a meal, she announced that next day we should be visiting the Tretiakov Museum, seeing the hall of icons among other things. In the hall of icons they had the two most beautiful icons in the world, Rublev's Trinity and Our Lady of Vladimar. I had the good fortune to spend some time once with an expatriate Russian theologian, Paul Evdokimov, an expert in iconography. In reply to my question, 'what is the most beautiful icon in the world?', he replied: 'You can choose between Our Lady of Vladimir and Rublev's Trinity; they are both at the peak.'

Now, before Our Lady of Vladimir, Lara excelled. She pointed out that it formerly hung in the church of the Assumption inside the Kremlin, that before it the Patriarchs were consecrated, the Czars crowned. As we left the room, I said to her: 'Lara, I think that you agree with what I said last evening on Red Square.' Again she just hung her head. A French woman who was in our group told me that in the bus on the way back to the hotel, Lara had spoken very frankly to her. She had got no religion. She felt that with socialism they must have religion. The Poles had got it right – though how many of the Poles were socialists was another question.

For our last night in Moscow they had laid on a special meal in a restaurant. As Lara led us to the entry, on my own behalf and on that of some Spanish priests who were in the group, I invited her to join us. She refused. I pressed her and then she gave the reason: her boyfriend was going on holidays next day, and she had to spend the last evening with him. I asked her if he was going to marry her. She didn't know; she hoped he wouldn't meet anyone! Then I said to her: 'Lara, I will pray that he marries you.' Her face lit up. Next day as we parted on the airport tarmac I reminded her of my promise. She told this to her colleague, and their happy laughter is my last memory of Moscow then.

VII

I was back in Moscow in October 1992, with the International Peace Pilgrimage organised by the 101 Foundation. This is the Moscow of the post-Gorbachev, post-Yeltsin initiatives, *glasnost, perestroika,* and the struggle for democracy. On the occasion of the 1966 visit I could not say Mass; in 1968 I did so, with another priest journalist, Michael Traber, Swiss, working in Northern Rhodesia (now Zimbabwe), but we had this privilege through the courtesy of a priest attached to an embassy; we said Mass in his private apartment.

Now in 1992 I was one of fifty concelebrants, with five bishops, in the auditorium of the Kosmos, a large hotel; all available seats were occupied. The Mass was the finale of an International Catholic Youth Congress (on the Alliance of the Two Hearts) which was given publicity with large notices in the lobbies and on the stairways of the hotel.

I saw many other signs of a new attitude to religion. I saw prayerful congregations on Sunday in the Patriarch's cathedral and in another smaller church. I was one of a group received by the Patriarch's delegate, an archbishop, to accept on his behalf an icon specially made for him – an icon of Our Lady of Fatima. This was the occasion of an exchange of gifts, the visitors receiving from the Orthodox prelate miniatures of the icon of Our Lady of Khazan; they were recipients too of warm thanks for the prayers offered over the years to Our Lady of Fatima for Russian Christians.

As a background to these happenings, I should mention that when the 101 Foundation pilgrimage reached Moscow airport, the statue of Our Lady of Fatima was borne across the tarmac from the plane to the terminal building, with a guard of honour formed by priests and bishops. On Sunday it was crowned in Red Square, at ten o'clock in the morning and at midnight.

For more ample information on the change following Gorbachev's visit to the Pope and the enactment of a charter of religious freedom, I commend the reader to the writings of an outstanding witness, Tatiana Goritcheva. She was expelled in the last of the bad days because of her active membership of *Maria*, the underground feminist movement – she had been demoted from a university lectureship to working a hotel elevator. She has gone back to find Russia athirst for God. Concomitant with such experience and testimony is a hugely symbolic event, the restoration to public worship of the three churches inside the Kremlin, of the Annunciation, the Assumption and St Michael; they had been preserved but as museums.

All this was in the future when I was in Moscow in 1968. Let me return to the narrative at that point. We went on to Budapest still under the shadow of the 'imprisoned' Cardinal. Here we met representatives of the Pax group, one of them a priest whom I had seen at the Berlin conference; he was allowed to leave Hungary, I should think, because he was a Pax member.

The poor man cut a pathetic figure at our Budapest meeting. In a brief survey of the politico-religious situation he belittled the Cardinal: 'He followed the American line.' I was moved to imprudence. I asked him how many Catholics were in jail, how many priests. No one, he replied, was imprisoned because of his or her religion. As to priests, yes there were some, but they had a 'martyr complex'. Yes, just that!

VIII

When we came out of this distressing encounter, one of the American priest journalists turned to me and said: 'If you're here much longer, they'll put you in jail.' That night in my room before going to bed, I suddenly felt a stab of cold terror. Had they bugged and taped the meeting? Were they talking about me? Was I safe through the presence of journalists from other countries? I sought the age-old solution, took out my rosary and said it as fervently as I could. I was very happy next day to board the plane for home.

The initial theme of these pages has been two Cardinals. I would like to end on a happy note. For Cardinal Mindszenty this is impossible. He has told in his memoirs how he suffered from ill-treatment from the church in the last phase of his life. He was persuaded to accept the deal made by Catholic authorities with the Hungarian government. He would regain his freedom without any compromise on his part. He was convinced that he would still retain his primatial position as Archbishop of Esztergom. It would appear that Paul VI was misled about the opinions of the Hungarian bishops, and decided to relieve the Cardinal of his office and appoint a successor. The sad thing was that if the Pope had waited a little longer, he would have spared the Cardinal the pain.

I met the Polish Cardinal twice before he died, at the International Marian Congress in Rome in 1975, when he invited me back to Poland, and in 1979 when I was in his country gathering material for a book on Poland and John Paul II. I went to greet his Eminence after the Sunday Mass in Warsaw cathedral. He was still in the afterglow of the election of a Polish Pope on a Polish feast-day, that of St Hedwig, on 16 October 1978. I said to the Cardinal that we hoped that John Paul II would come to Ireland later in the year; the occasion would be the centenary of the apparition at Knock. Would the Cardinal ever think of accompanying him? 'Ah,' he said humourously, 'he has left me alone here. I can't leave.'

When the papal visit had taken place, I was able to obtain a video of the highlights. I had it sent to Rome with a view to having it eventually delivered to the Cardinal. To my very great delight, when the Pope heard of it, he had it sent in his own name.

In January 1979 I was taken by a monk from Czestochowa to the archiepiscopal residence in Cracow. There I saw the large image of Our Lady of Czestochowa given by Wyszyinski to

Wojtyla, when the latter was appointed to the see of Cracow. It was in the Oratory where the future Pope often came to work, as well as to pray.

I heard the story of an enlightening episode. What, I asked the sister who was our guide, was his reaction to the news of John Paul I's death? Through the interpreter she told me. He was at breakfast in a small room which she pointed out; it was near the kitchen. At the news, he put his head in his hands and just said: 'Jesu, Maria, what will happen now?' He knew.

The Cardinal died on 28 May 1981, just a fortnight and a day after the assassination attempt on the Pope, 13 May. There was a last poignant moment when John Paul had a telephone call from his friend in Warsaw, the dying man talking to the one snatched miraculously from death. What a grace to the church they both have been!

15. John Paul II

I

John Paul II is already the second longest reigning Pope in the present century; only Pius XII, who reigned for nineteen years and seven months, had a longer pontificate. No one can deny that the decade and nine years through which the church has lived since 16 October 1978, the day of his election, have been important. Nor can anyone deny that his pontificate has been distinctive. He has travelled more throughout the church not only than any of his predecessors, but than all of them together; he recently logged his millionth kilometre. I am not writing as his apologist. For those who love and admire him, as I do – and I have met such people in the five continents – there is no need for an apologist. With those who neither love nor admire him, no apologist would have much success. Let us stay with the facts. I am concerned because as a journalist I have frequently written of him; I have composed two books on his life and teaching. When, at public meetings in many countries, I have expressed my loyalty to him I have met enthusiastic applause.

John Paul II was, on his election as Pope, a man of intellectual stature. He was the author of five books and one hundred and ninety articles in reviews; articles in the press are not included in the figure. His intellectual interests spanned from St John of the Cross, mystical theology, to Max Scheler's phenomenology; in each he had written a substantial academic dissertation; a dictionary of philosophy has included an entry under his name, noting fifty published items. Shortly after his election his old Roman university, the Angelico, brought out a special number of its review, *Angelicum*, devoted exclusively to a study of his thought;

nine contributors dealt with different aspects of his published work. This showed that the Pope, not yet sixty, had, besides assuring the administration and pastoral care of a large diocese, furnished a very considerable intellectual output.

The future Pope had spoken eleven times during the Second Vatican Council. He had published a profound analysis of its teaching in book form. A few years ago, Cardinal de Lubac, an important theologian of the Council, wrote in the weekly, *La France Catholique*, that the young Bishop Wojtyla had so impressed him during the Council sessions that he thought him *papabile*.

I cannot include in my personal memoirs any notable events in which the Pope figures. I did have the great joy of concelebrating Mass with him in his private oratory on a day in January 1981. I had met Mgr (now Bishop) Magee, his secretary and Master of Ceremonies, in St Peter's Square and he asked me if I would like to do so. Would I? The Pope was photographed with each of us individually afterwards. Among the others present was a French priest whom I very much admire, Marie Dominique Philippe, OP, founder of an admirable society of priests. We spoke of a mutual acquaintance, Fr François Marie Braun, OP, a biblical scholar. Yes, he told me, he was dead. 'Our Lady took him on her feast day, the Assumption.' Four months later the assassination attempt on John Paul II took place. We now know that the Pope considers his escape from death a miracle.

About this time I took down the *Insegnamenti*, the complete collection of papal texts, spoken and written, which is issued annually. I made a rough cast-off of matter published for the year 1980; I reckoned that the Pope had published then over a million words in seven languages. That is the equivalent of five substantial books. The output diminished understandably in the year 1981, but it was soon back to the same level, if not higher.

The precise original authorship of each of these texts is not known. A Pope cannot undertake the research and composition that go into each encyclical, apostolic exhortation or lesser papal document. He indicates the subject, chooses the writer, who presumably may consult others. He may suggest broad treatment, review the final draft and alter it as he thinks wise. It is said that

Pope John Paul II wrote his first encyclical, *Redemptor Hominis*, personally; this is not known with certainty. Over the years, like many interested in the papacy, I have heard the name of one theologian or another mentioned in regard to a particular encyclical, for example Fr (later Cardinal) Augustine Bea, SJ, of the Biblical institute for Pius XII's epoch-making encyclical on the Bible, *Divino Afflante Spiritu*, Mgr Pavan of the Lateran University for John XIII's very influential encyclical, *Pacem in Terris.*

John Paul's twelve encyclicals make a substantial corpus, which will be required reading for students of Catholic teaching. As Pius XII is the most frequently quoted authority outside the Bible in the documents of Vatican II, John Paul II figures very largely in the annotation of the *Catechism of the Catholic Church*. In assessing his role as teacher, one must take account of a vast number of other documents, papal or apostolic letters, formal addresses or messages, the carefully written texts which make up his Wednesday catecheses, and his annual Holy Thursday letter to priests.

Especially enlightening are the apostolic exhortations which are based on the findings and recommendations of episcopal synods called to deal with matters of relevance to the contemporary church: *Catechesi Tradendae* on the teaching of religion, *Familiaris Consortio* on family life, *Pastores dabo Vobis* on priestly formation, *Christifideles Laici* on the laity, *Ecclesia in Africa* on the church in Africa, the great success story in modern missionary history.

II

Will any of John Paul's encyclicals stand high above the flow of church teaching like, for example Leo XIII's *Rerum Novarum*, Pius XII's *Divino Afflante Spiritu*, or John XXIII's *Pacem in Terris*? I should be prompted to pick out *Dominum et Vivificantem* on the Holy Spirit or *Evangelium Vitae* on the sanctity of life. The first is the most important statement on the Holy Spirit to come from the papacy, and the Holy Spirit is the one who answers the deepest yearning of the Christian world at the present time; the second deals with the overwhelming disease of the twentieth century, the culture of death. One must not overlook the innovation of John Paul II, his decision to publish a book answering questions put to him by a journalist, *The Threshold of Hope*, universally translated, a world bestseller. He also wrote for publication a work linked with his priestly golden jubilee.

What are the great themes of the Pope's teaching? First I would choose the Holy Spirit. Not only in the encyclical but in countless other writings or addresses, he has given a body of reflection and instruction which in quantity and quality surpasses what any single one of his predecessors has given us. The reader who finds this assertion excessive may begin by looking at the following items: the chapter in the encyclical *Redemptoris Missio* on the Holy Spirit as the principal agent of mission – it brings to a satisfactory conclusion the outline in the Decree of Vatican II and in Paul VI's *Evangelii Nuntiandi*; the illuminating series of Wednesday catecheses on the subject in 1991; the letter to priests likewise; the passage on charisms among the laity in *Christifideles Laici* – an idea to which he returns in other addresses; and many other interesting reflections given as the occasion warranted.

All this is the answer to Paul VI's call to theologians and preachers to add to the theology of the church and of Our Lady given by Vatican II, a theology of the Holy Spirit. The Pope was reacting favourably to the call of a representative Orthodox theologian, Nikos Nissiotis, who in trenchant articles told the Council fathers that, if they did not include a satisfactory doctrine of the Holy Spirit in their documents, these would have no impact in the Orthodox world – there the Holy Spirit is paramount.

III

As Pope, John Paul II has been faithful to the powerful Marian tradition of his people. He summarised his thought in the encyclical, *Redemptoris Mater*, 1987. He has visited her shrines all over the world, thereby affirming his solidarity with the People of God. There is no important document bearing his signature, no telling address, wherein he fails to show the essential relevance of the Mother of God to each and every aspect and need of the Christian life. He first used the phrase 'Alliance of the Two Hearts' and, with a formal letter and an official address, he was at one with the participants in the symposium held in Fatima in 1986 on this theme. At Fatima in 1982, when he thanked Our Lady for saving him from death in the attempted assassination, he spoke words of consecration. On 25 March 1984, in Rome, after informing the hierarchy of the whole church of his intention, he formally consecrated the church and the world to the Immaculate Heart of Mary. When the Bishop of Fatima thanked him for the consecration of the world, he replied 'And Russia.' With Pius XII he is the outstanding Marian Pope of modern times. He has encouraged the movement which requests a definition of the dogma of Mary, Co-Redemptress, Mediatress of all graces, Advocate.

John Paul II has spoken on every grave problem of our time. What has been the effect in the world of the action of his papal office? Gorbachev paid him an immense tribute: if there had not been a Slav Pope the marxist regimes in Russia and eastern Europe would not have crumbled. Gorbachev invited him to visit Russia, but tensions between Patriarch Alexei II and the Catholic bishops, one an archbishop, rendered this, for the time being, unhelpful. This circumstance may also explain the fact that the Pope did not mention Russia explicitly in his act of consecration to the Immaculate Heart of Mary. Let us hope for the future.

In two continuing policies John Paul will be remembered. He has made every effort possible to maintain and strengthen the ties between the Catholic Church and the Orthodox. Annually, since the time of the previous Ecumenical Patriarch, Dimitrios I, delegations go to Istanbul for the feast of St Andrew, and come to Rome for the feast of SS Peter and Paul. These culminated, on 29 June 1995, in a visit of the present Patriarch, Bartholomew I to Rome.

John Paul II was the first Pope to visit the Jewish synagogue in Rome, saying: 'It has taken two thousand years to cross the two kilometres which separate us.' He received in audience

Israeli ministers of state, Shimon Peres as Foreign Minister and Prime Minister, Ishztak Rabin. In particular, he initiated and supported the negotiations which led to the Fundamental Agreement between the Vatican and the State of Israel. Not too long ago theologians could be found who would have declared such an undertaking forbidden. I have written and spoken so much in praise of St Pius X that I hope that he will forgive me for referring to something not so flattering of him. Theodore Herzl, founder of the Zionist movement, the object of which was to secure a homeland for the Jews in Palestine, asked the Pope for a blessing on his endeavour; it was refused. We have come a long way since then. We learned a great deal from the Holocaust. John Paul II lived not far away from Auschwitz, went there to ponder its mystery, and went there as Pope to say Mass in the presence of survivors, including the one who owed his life to St Maxmillian Kolbe.

IV

I have been present at public papal ceremonies, such as the Beatification of two members of my own congregation. Blessed Jacques Désiré Laval, apostle of the island of Mauritius, and Blessed Daniel Brottier, a missionary of whom I have written. I was with the participants in the symposium on the Alliance of the Two Hearts when the Pope met us, and accepted a complete typescript of all the contributions, and the Votum, that is a request that he give papal expression to our findings – he had already commissioned the Encyclical *Redemptoris Mater*, which impeded things. I also assisted at the public consistory when my friend Paul Poupard was promoted to the Sacred College; I had known him when he came to stay with us in Blackrock College; at the time he was Rector of the Catholic Institute in Paris.

On 24 May 1995, as I have said, I had the great joy of concelebrating with the Pope in his private oratory. I met the Pope briefly after the Mass and presented to him my second book on Vassula Ryden, in French translation; I had given him a copy of the first in the course of an audience in November 1993. This time the Pope asked me two questions: Is she Orthodox? Is she married? Then he told me to consult Cardinal Ratzinger. I was awaiting a dossier which Patrick Beneston was preparing, before seeking an interview with His Eminence, when the Notification about Vassula appeared in the *Osservatore Romano*. I have dealt with this publication and the worldwide sequel in *Vassula and Rome*.

On the same day, 24 May, Fr René Laurentin was also a concelebrant at the Papal Mass. He was beside me when the Pope came to speak to each of the concelebrants. With no previous agreement he also was presenting to the Pope his second book on Vassula. When the Pope asked him quite simply: 'What do you think of her?', part of his reply was: 'She is much calumniated.'

After the appearance of the Notification, I went as president of the Association based on Vassula's writings, *True Life in God*, to plead her cause in Rome. Again, in a few moments, after the General Wednesday audience, 29 November, I spoke to the Pope about Vassula. I said: 'You told me last May to contact Cardinal Ratzinger. This I am doing.' I asked him for a blessing for Vassula and this he gave. He signed the cross on my forehead and spoke a confidential word to me. I felt that I was in the presence of one of the greatest saints in the history of the world. Cardinal Ratzinger was absent from Rome. I deposed two immense dossiers in his office in care of two prelates with whom I spoke, one dossier dealing with testimonies and matters prior to the Notification, the other with all that was sent to us after it appeared. On 5 December I saw Patriarch Bartholomew I in London. He was aware of what had been done to a member of his church, in violation of the Balamand Declaration.

What does the future hold for John Paul II? It would be idle to deny that there are many prophecies circulating about him. I have seen or heard a number of these. One thing is certain: God is very, very near him and has set on him the seal of pre-eminent predestination.

16. The Orthodox

I feel a serious obligation to acquire and to diffuse knowledge of the Orthodox Church. The first reason, which scarcely needs to be explained, is ecumenical in the full sense of that word. If Christians are to be united they must begin by coming to know each other. Such knowledge must be not only of theory, of doctrine, but of those who in our time interpret and live the doctrine.

I believe, moreover, that Catholic ecumenists have somewhat neglected the Orthodox. So much attention was given to Protestants that there was little time for the separated brethren of the east. Yet, as has so often been said authoritatively in recent times, what unites us with them is far more important that what divides us. One who has said that, John Paul II, is my third reason for giving special attention to Orthodoxy and to its present head, Bartholomew I, *primus inter pares* of the Orthodox Patriarchs. The Pope has done more than any of his predecessors to prepare for unity with the Orthodox, unity which, he is convinced, will be especially the work of the Holy Spirit. In that expectation he has spiritual kinship with them, for he is the Pope of the Holy Spirit.

When I got the suggestion of doing a book on Bartholomew, I thought it my duty to seek his authorisation. After some odd vicissitudes I reached Istanbul on 1 November 1994. I was fortunate to meet him in the Phanar, the official patriarchal residence. I could guess his puzzlement at the request of a Catholic priest living far from the east, outside his ecclesial communion. I was able to reassure him, to let him know that I had studied Orthodoxy, in its history and theology, and members of his church, particularly in Russia, Greece, Romania.

I told the Patriarch that I had to be back in Dublin in about a week for the blessing of the first Orthodox church – until then the Divine Liturgy had been celebrated in borrowed churches. 'I believe the Pastor is Romanian,' said Bartholomew I. 'He's a friend of mine; we discussed his doctorate on Mary and the Holy Trinity,' I replied: 'I was invited to act on the examining jury that awarded him his degree.' That settled it. The Orthodox priest in question was the first of his church to obtain a doctorate in our national Pontifical University, Fr Ireneu Cracian.

Fr Tarasios, the Patriarch's deacon, gave me valuable documentation and from a friend in the World Council of Churches I received further interesting items. I subscribed to the Paris based *Service Orthodoxe de Presse* which covers Bartholomew's activities continuously. With the weekly edition of *L'Osservatore Romano* one has abundant information. A problem with my subject is the magnitude of his achievement in word and action. He is fluent in six languages, and has had a brilliant academic career. In the United States I met an Orthodox priest who had been a fellow student with him in the Halki Institute of Theology. All of them, he assured me, thought him the intellectual leader.

He owed his schooling largely to a remarkable Orthodox prelate, Metropolitan Meliton, Archbishop of Imbros and Tenedos, his spiritual father. Possibly through his influence the young student came to the notice of the great Athenagoras, who gave him a bursary to facilitate study abroad. As he was interested in church law, he opted first for the Pontifical Oriental Institute in Rome, attached to the Gregorian University. While in Rome he stayed in the Séminaire Français, which is staffed by members of my congregation. Here he met the elite of French seminarians, some of whom have since become bishops.

Already responsive to the ideas of Athenagoras, he became more so in his Roman years, for his stay coincided with the Second Vatican Council. For the first time in centuries, members of the Orthodox Church were present at a General Council of the Catholic Church; they were Observers, without the right of direct participation in the conciliar debates or in voting, but with the power of lobbying. The young student from the east may not have been as excited as were his Latin classmates and peers; he could not escape the contagion altogether. In the very house where he lived, the Séminaire Français, there was an important conciliar figure, Père Joseph Lécuyer, the outstanding theologian of the priesthood, a specialist in the conciliar theme of collegiality, and secretary of the commission for priests.

The future Patriarch went on to study at the Bossey Institute of Theology, situated in Geneva under the aegis of the World Council of Churches; he completed his academic phase in the University of Munich. His proficiency can be measured by his Roman doctorate thesis, which has since been published, on *The Codification of the Holy Canons and the Canonical Constitutions in the Orthodox Church*. Travel had sharpened his linguistic skill. Though without a word of Latin when he arrived in Rome, he went through his examinations in that language within a matter of months; in Munich he acquired German.

His academic attainments and his personal qualities brought him close to the prelate who in 1972 succeeded the deceased Athenagoras, Dimitrios I. He worked with and for him, travelled with him, shared his ecumenical programme. Dimitrios had welcomed John Paul II to the Phanar in Istanbul, and had himself visited the Pope in Rome. With John Paul II he had initiated the annual visits of important delegations to Istanbul from the Vatican for the patronal feast of St Andrew and from Istanbul to Rome for the feast of SS Peter and Paul. The Pope and the Patriarch had also set up a joint Roman Catholic Orthodox theological commission.